THE TUDORS

PERSONALITIES AND PRACTICAL
POLITICS IN SIXTEENTH
CENTURY ENGLAND

By CONYERS READ

The Norton Library

W · W · NORTON & COMPANY · INC ·
NEW YORK

60-872-570

Books That Live
The Norton imprint on a book means that in the publisher's
estimation it is a book not for a single season but for the years.
W. W. Norton & Company, Inc.

PREFACE

This book is designed to give a brief survey of the history of England under the Tudors. It is addressed to those of college age or older. No attempt has been made to fit it to classroom requirements, though it may serve as collateral reading for college courses in English history or English literature. I trust it will be found readable by a wider reading public. There is undoubtedly a good deal of history being read by those who are outside the academic walls. Much of it is written by scribes who have no other qualifications for the task than an easy hand with the pen and a keen nose for the sensational and the salacious. So it is that Henry VIII is remembered rather for the multitude of his wives than for his solid contribution to the progress of England, and Elizabeth rather for her flirtations than for her statescraft. The fault lies at the door of the historians who are qualified to speak with authority. They have, by and large, ignored the demands of the reading public and have confined their literary endeavors to the writing of learned monographs addressed to a very small and very erudite circle of readers. Not all of them to be sure have the art to present their subject in terms which will interest the casual reader. But many who have are deterred by a prevalent professional sentiment that it is a little undignified to shape the findings of scholarship to the popular taste. There is no sound reason why good history should not be as interesting as bad history, except that good historians, most of whom are more or less comfortably settled in college chairs, can afford to be dull, whereas bad historians, who have to live by their wits, must find a supporting reading public or starve. In any case, I believe that historians should assume a certain responsibility for dispensing sound history to the people at large, and should not abandon history as it is read to the tender mercies of publicans and sinners.

I have spent a large part of my life in thinking and speaking and writing about Tudor history. This book represents my conclusions about the matter. It lacks all the obvious paraphernalia of scholarship but I think it reflects pretty accurately the findings of sound scholars upon the subjects under consideration. I hope it will prove palatable to those who, under no compulsion from academic disciplines, may read it or not as they choose.

It was intended originally for the Berkshire

Studies in European History, but it turned out to be too long for that admirable series and the editors, Richard A. Newhall, Laurence B. Packard, and Sidney R. Packard, have been good enough to consent to its appearance in its present form.

It has been written at odd intervals in a very busy professional life, and it could hardly have been written at all without the devoted coöperation of my assistant, Evelyn Plummer Braun, who has not only criticized and corrected the manuscript and seen it through the press but has also taken many unpleasant tasks upon her own shoulders so that I might have spare time for the writing of it. I acknowledge my debt to her with gratitude.

C. R.

University of Pennsylvania
January, 1936.

CONTENTS

ILLUSTRATIONS

facing page

[xi]

THE TUDORS

HENRY VII

CHAPTER I

HENRY VII

ENRY VII, first of the Tudor monarchs, won his throne by conquest
in 1485 on Bosworth Field. His
father Edmund Tudor was a Welsh
gentleman, of royal Welsh lineage,
a matter of relatively little importance in English
eyes though it strengthened Henry's position
among the Welsh. What claim he had to the English crown by birthright he derived from his
mother, Margaret Beaufort, a descendant by the
back stairs through John of Gaunt from Edward
III. In the warring factions of York and Lancaster that harried England before his accession
he belongs therefore among the Lancastrians.
From them, in his struggle for the throne, he derived his chief strength. His hereditary claim was,
however, ignored in the parliamentary confirmation of his title and was probably regarded in his
time as of doubtful validity. He contrived to
strengthen it somewhat, later, by his marriage to
Elizabeth, heiress of the Yorkist claims. But the

matter was really decided on Bosworth Field.

Henry's pedigree gave him his opportunity but he won his crown by patience, cunning and sheer hard fighting. The important factor was the quality of the man, not the validity of his title. This indeed may be said of the Tudors in general. The England which goes by their name would have been a far different England without them. They were leaders of their people as probably no English sovereigns have been before or since. On that account their personal attributes are matters of first-rate importance. The remarkable thing about Henry was not that he was a strong king or even that he was a wise king, but the character of his strength and his wisdom. He was the product of an age of feudal disorder and by every reckoning ought to have been thoroughly saturated with the habits of thought and behavior of his time. Yet in all essential characteristics he was as remote from the prepossessions and inhibitions of feudal England as Machiavelli was. It is apparent from the outset that he broke sharply and deliberately with the whole feudal scheme of things, saw in the nobles of his own class and station the great menace to a strong state and set up his rest upon the bourgeois standards of the townsfolk. He was, of course, not alone in that position. Strong monarchs

elsewhere had reached substantially the same conclusion at substantially the same time. But Henry
had had no chance to observe the difficulties at-
tendant upon the feudal conception of monarchy
at close range. He had never been heir apparent,
or even heir presumptive. He had been a poor,
struggling pretender, with a price upon his head,
until the fortunes of war made him king.

The man stands forth against the background
of the Wars of the Roses a curiously modern figure, almost, one might say, the first of the moderns
among English monarchs. The chroniclers who described his appearance on Bosworth Field spoke
of his countenance "cheerful and courageous," his
hair "like burnished gold," his eyes "gray, shining
and quick" and felt it necessary to apologize for
the fact that he was of no great stature; in a word
did their best to make a conventional medieval
champion of Henry. But the more familiar and
more convincing picture is that by an unknown
Flemish artist which reveals a shrewd, hard face,
wide-open eyes, a mouth tight shut with a quizzi-
cal smile lurking at the corners, such a smile as
Leonardo loved to paint. What the man lacked
apparently was any personal charm. They called
his son later Bluff King Hal and his granddaughter Good Queen Bess, but none ever gave

Henry VII a nickname. He never seems to have caught the popular imagination. What contemporaries chiefly remarked in him was his wisdom, by which they meant his sound common sense. Men feared him, admired him, depended upon him, but they did not love him.

Henry's problem was that of restoring the strength of the monarchy. For thirty years the crown had been the plaything of the opposing factions of Lancaster and York. He had to set it above faction. If we were to single out the two guiding principles of his reign they would be to curb the power of the nobles and to strengthen the power of the middle classes. So far as the nobles were concerned, he inherited a tradition from the Wars of the Roses that kings were set up to be knocked down. He had this advantage, however, over his predecessors, that the supply of alternatives for the throne had been considerably diminished. Among possible Lancastrian candidates he had easily the best claim. His marriage to Elizabeth of York did something to satisfy the pretensions of the Yorkists, but there were two elements in that party which were quite irreconcilable. One of these was the Geraldine family in Ireland who controlled the English government—so far as it could be called a government—there. The other was

Margaret, Edward IV's sister, the widow of Charles the Bold of Burgundy. Ireland was the hatchery of almost every plot against the throne which Henry VII had to face and Margaret the patron saint. The Yorkists suffered from the lack of any satisfactory candidate for the succession. Edward IV's two sons had been murdered, though that fact was not yet established. He had four surviving nephews, one his brother's son, known as the Earl of Warwick, the other three the sons of his sister by John de la Pole, Earl of Suffolk. Warwick had the strongest claim, probably on the grounds of heredity alone, a better claim than Henry himself, but he was only ten years old and a prisoner in the Tower. The oldest of the de la Poles was barely twenty-one. That explains why the Yorkists pinned their hopes to charlatans, posing now as the Earl of Warwick, now as one of the murdered sons of Edward IV. The unfortunate part about this device was that the charlatans had to be mere boys in order to sustain their rôles. Their selection appears to have been made rather haphazard. The two most conspicuous of them, Lambert Simnel and Perkin Warbeck, commanded considerable support, not only from Yorkists in England and Ireland, but from Scotland, Burgundy and other enemies of England overseas.

Simnel, assisted by the oldest of the de la Pole nephews, was able to raise a sizable army, chiefly of Irishmen and German mercenaries, and to give battle to Henry at Stoke. The king won after a hard fight, de la Pole was killed, Simnel pardoned and made a scullion in the royal kitchen. It was a disdainful gesture and so far as Simnel himself was concerned, probably a fair appraisal of his ability, but the attempt itself was a rather grim jest. Four years later Perkin Warbeck, a young Flemish impostor, was induced to assume a similar rôle. His public career started likewise in Ireland and for six years his attempts to build up a party against Henry led him from court to court in Europe. Everywhere he found a friendly reception and, excepting perhaps in Spain, a recognition of his pretensions. He was responsible for a Scottish invasion from the north and a Cornish rebellion in the west and he weakened Henry's diplomatic position in Europe considerably. In the end he failed and died a traitor's death, but his whole performance, like that of Simnel before him, bears eloquent testimony to the instability of Henry's position. When callow charlatans could breed so much disturbance one wonders what would have happened had the Yorkists been able to produce a real leader with a genuine claim to consideration. There were other pretenders to follow. Another one of the de la Poles disturbed Henry's peace and distorted his diplomacy during the closing years of his reign. But with Warbeck's death, accompanied as it was by the execution of the captive Earl of Warwick on a trumped-up charge of conspiracy, the real menace to Henry's position from internal rebellion passed.

He realized, however, that so long as the restless nobles were allowed to gather their retainers about them unchecked, civil peace was in jeopardy. And civil peace was imperative, not only because disturbance was the breeding ground of rebellion, but also because the establishment of good order was the surest vindication of Henry's own right to rule and the strongest possible bid for the continued support of the bourgeoisie. In this connection the abuses which cried loudest for correction were those of livery and maintenance; maintenance by the nobility of armed retainers and the informal enlistment of large bands of cut-throats by the simple expedient of distributing to them some badge or livery. These practices had been forbidden more than once by law, but it was perfectly apparent that the ordinary courts were powerless to deal with the retainers of the greater nobles. What jury in the north would dare to bring in a verdict against a

follower of the Nevilles or the Percys? Henry's
first parliament revived the old legislation and
Henry undertook to give it vitality by exacting
from every member of the House of Lords an
oath to support it. But he presently went further
than that. The judicial powers of his Council were
wide and indefinite. It was in theory the fountain-
head of royal justice and the residuary legatee of
all judicial powers not expressly conferred upon
the other royal courts. Henry utilized this fact to
reorganize it, strengthened it by the addition of
the two chief justices and secured from parliament
in 1487 a law giving it special jurisdiction in all
cases of livery, maintenance or civil disorder. This
law came to be known as the Star Chamber Act
and this court as the Court of Star Chamber. In
essence it was not new. The powers conferred in
1487 were powers already inherent, the personnel
was still the councilors of the king. What was new
was the emphasis and the more precise definition
of powers not clearly defined and more or less
in abeyance. The peculiar potency of Star Chamber
lay in the facts that its personnel was under
Henry's direct control, that it functioned under
his eye and that its procedure, though public, dis-
pensed with the forms of common law. There was
no jury, there might be torture to compel testi-

mony. It was entirely free, therefore, from local prejudices and local fears. Naturally it was unpopular among the restless nobility and looked at askance by the custodians of the common law. But during the sixteenth century it was generally regarded by the common people as a great bulwark of defense against the tyranny of the nobles. Its unpopularity dates from the seventeenth century when its real work had been done and the king and his people were in opposite camps.

The net result of the Star Chamber Act was vastly to increase, in fact if not in theory, the power of the king's privy council in all matters pertaining to public order. It was the first of several laws enacted by Tudor parliaments, the cumulative effect of which was to concentrate in the hands of the council supreme power not only in civil, but ultimately also, in ecclesiastical government. In this respect as in so many others Henry VII indicated the course of Tudor policy. But if he was intent to increase the power of his council he was equally intent that his council should remain the docile instrument of his will. He abandoned therefore the feudal conception of a council composed of great vassals with hereditary rights and large feudal resources to support those rights. His councilors were his creatures, selected for their ability,

selected above all for their loyalty. Those whom
he trusted most were all of them men of humble
or at best indifferent origin. And this was true of
all the great Tudor statesmen who followed. If a
great nobleman remained in the council at all he
played an obscure part, and if he aspired to a large
part he was in danger of the judgment. Bucking-
ham fell for that sin in the reign of Henry's son
and Norfolk in the reign of his granddaughter. It
was just as dangerous to seek an independent
source of strength, from the church as Wolsey did,
or from popular support, which was probably the
head and front of Essex's offending under Elizabeth. The Tudor statesmen who survived and who
flourished set up their rest solely upon their
prince's favor. It speaks volumes, however, for the
wisdom of the Tudors that they were intolerant of
mere sycophants. Their agents might be unpopular—it was probably in the line of their interests to be unpopular—but they were competent
men almost without exception.

The actual organization of the royal privy council is relatively unimportant, for the time was yet
far distant when we can speak of any elaborate
civil service or any precise distribution of powers
and responsibilities among the several councilors.
They had, of course, official titles and a definite

order of procedure, but in the actual operation of the government this meant little or nothing. The Tudors were more concerned about getting things done than about who did them. Generally speaking the principal secretary was the chief administrative official, at least after Wolsey's fall. Thomas Cromwell, Stephen Gardiner, William Cecil, Francis Walsingham and Robert Cecil all held that office. There were, however, other principal secretaries who were little better than superior clerks. It all depended upon the man himself. Under Henry VII no minister ever assumed a position of commanding importance. Henry was his own prime minister, and so, after Wolsey's fall, was his son Henry VIII and so throughout her reign was Elizabeth, his granddaughter. The other two Tudors, Edward and Mary, had short reigns and neither of them can fairly be regarded as normal specimens of their breed.

The financial problem was the most difficult as it was probably the most important one which Henry VII had to face. He recognized that himself and as soon as he felt fairly secure upon his throne he devoted a large part of his attention to it. In consequence he called down upon his head a great deal of opprobrium both then and since. No doubt he did become obsessed, towards the end of his reign, with the mere business of accumulating wealth. Men who devote themselves exclusively to that occupation frequently do. Nevertheless, Henry's objective was a sound one. The fundamental weakness of the feudal monarch had always been his financial dependence upon his vassals. Outside of the income from his own lands the feudal king commanded no assured sources of royal revenue. Some little came to him from the estates of royal wards and from the sale of their hands in marriage; some more by the appropriation of the lands of royal vassals who died without heirs or who were condemned traitors. He could also on rare occasions collect certain so-called feudal aids for specified extraordinary expenses, such as the knighting of his eldest son, the marriage of his eldest daughter and the ransom of his body from captivity. And there were fees from the sale of royal writs and fines collected in the courts of royal justice, besides odds and ends of various sorts. But all these taken together were inadequate to the uses of the new monarchy. What the king needed besides he had to get if he could by appeal to his subjects, that is to say, from parliament. But this appeal was held to be justified only by some extraordinary emergency, such as a foreign war. It was part of the theory of the feudal régime that the king's income from his personal estates was sufficient to meet his normal requirements—otherwise put, the king should live upon his own.

Henry discovered early that "his own" was not enough, but he realized also that appeals to parliament for money, except for popular enterprises, would weaken his position with the very class to which he looked for strength. For although parliament was still in theory an assembly of the king's vassals, the element in it which supplied the money was the middle class, sitting in the house of commons. This middle class was well inclined to sit by and give Henry its moral support in his efforts to break the power of the old nobility, but was not so ready to finance the venture. It was Henry's problem, therefore, to increase his revenues on the one hand without alienating the commons by heavy taxes on the other. That in essence was the major problem of all the Tudors and that was why Henry preferred to scrape all his established sources of revenue to the bone and to extort money under all sorts of false pretenses from individuals before he resorted to general taxes. Much of what he did to increase his income was no more than to get rid of a lot of corruption and inefficiency in his fiscal organization. He saw to it that what was due him was collected and paid into his treasury. He reaped a rich harvest also by wholesale confiscation of the property of political offenders. He got money from the church by allowing ecclesiastical offices in his appointment to remain vacant and pocketing their revenues in the interim. His profits from the administration of justice were perhaps the shadiest of all. These are associated with the names of Richard Empson and Edmund Dudley. Both of these men were lawyers and both were employed by Henry in the business of searching out all sorts of breaches of forgotten laws and imposing fines accordingly. How much of this was justifiable, how much simply a thinly disguised method of extortion, it is not easy to say. It was directed in the main against the old nobility and so served the double purpose of increasing the king's treasure and depleting the resources of his opponents. There can be no doubt that Henry himself directed the efforts of his agents. A memorandum book of Dudley's survives with copious annotations in the king's own hand.

The customs duties supplied another important source of revenue which stood midway between royal and parliamentary control. They consisted chiefly of specific duties on the export of wool and on the import of wine and *ad valorem* duties upon the import and export of merchandise. The wine duty and the merchandise duty usually go by the name of tunnage and poundage. All these customs duties were well established, were theoretically granted by parliament, but beginning with the reign of Edward IV were conferred upon the king for life. The rates were fixed by law and the resulting revenues were consequently beyond the king's control except in so far as his commercial policy operated to increase or decrease the volume of foreign trade. But the *ad valorem* duty was naturally governed by the valuations placed upon the commodities subject to duty. These were originally made by the merchants themselves under oath. In 1507, however, Henry substituted for this procedure an official valuation known as a Book of Rates and so opened the door to an arbitrary alteration of values by the crown for the purpose of increasing revenues, which was to make trouble later. The return from the customs formed under Henry VII at least a quarter of his total revenues. And it can not be doubted that no small part of his interest in trade arose out of the prospect of increasing his income from that source. In actual figures the increase during his reign amounted to about 30 per cent, from a little over £30,000 at the beginning of his reign to a little over £40,000 at the end.

Parliamentary grants of money were intended to meet extraordinary emergencies, notably foreign wars. Henry did not attempt to break with tradition in this regard though there is evidence to prove that he made wars to give him an excuse for raising money quite as often as he raised money for the sake of waging war. In general his wars paid for themselves and yielded a comfortable profit. Taxes took the conventional form of a so-called Tenth and Fifteenth, or a multiple of the same. Theoretically they were taxes upon the capital value of movable property, a tenth in the towns, a fifteenth in the country. Actually, however, a single Tenth and Fifteenth represented a parliamentary grant of about £35,000, which was apportioned throughout England as it had been ever since 1334, a fixed amount from each district, levied and collected by local collectors. Exactly how these collectors determined their assessments is far from clear, but it is certain that they made no exact appraisal of personal property and that the conventional fractions, tenth and fifteenth, meant nothing. In consequence the yield of the tax did not respond to the growing wealth of the country. Its one merit was that the people were

accustomed to it. At a time when the whole idea
of taxation was still in its infancy this was a consideration of no small importance. Henry was well
aware of its shortcomings; he was also well aware
that taxes of any sort were unpopular and he believed it wiser to proceed along customary lines
than to attempt new devices. The efforts of his
predecessors in that direction had not been re-
assuring. His son after him tried to install a more
equitable plan of assessment but without success.
This much at least can be said for Tudor taxes,
that they fell alike on noble and simple, exempted
the very poor and in general were paid by those
best able to bear them. There were no oppressive
excises on the necessities of life like the salt tax
in France.

Henry resorted at times to direct extortion from
his richer subjects by compelling them to make
personal contributions to his necessities under the
name of what were politely called benevolences.
They were unpopular with those upon whom they
were imposed but were probably regarded by the
people at large as a very acceptable alternative
to a parliamentary tax. The forced loans of his
son and the so-called privy seals of Elizabeth belong to the same category, though the Elizabethan
privy seals were both in form and in effect con-

tractual obligations, extracted to be sure under pressure, but invariably repaid.

The net result of Henry's financial policy was a steady accumulation of treasure. How large this treasure was at his death is not accurately known. Sir Francis Bacon's guess was £1,800,000. A Venetian ambassador, reporting in 1531, put the figure at £1,300,000. Contemporary gossip made Henry out to be richer "than well-nigh all the other kings of Christendom." This much is certain that he left behind him at his death a considerable fortune, though the available evidence indicates that this fortune was rather in the form of jewels, plate and accounts receivable than in actual ready money.

It is not surprising to discover that Henry took a keen interest in the development of English trade. His steady emphasis upon the development of his resources led him, if for no other reason, to promote the interests of the moneyed classes in his kingdom. English exports were for the most part in raw wool and in woolen cloth. The wool found a ready market in the Low Countries and in Italy. For the cloth there was a wide demand. The bulk of English trade flowed to the Low Countries and to the Mediterranean, though there was a considerable trade with the wine-growing regions in western France, some with Spain and some with the Baltic countries. For the most part this trade was carried by the ships of the Hansa league and by the Venetian galleys. Henry VII had two clear purposes in mind in his attitude towards trade—one to increase the volume of it, the other to encourage the growth of English shipping. To some extent one operated to defeat the other, for in so far as Henry imposed restrictions upon foreign carriers in the interests of English ones, his policy tended to reduce the shipping available to English exporters and so to reduce the volume of English trade. He was shrewd enough to see this and for that reason his so-called navigation policy was never consistently carried forward. We must not allow ourselves to be misguided by his legislation on the subject. Tudor legislation on this point as on all other points is never a safe guide to actual policy. Laws, regulative and restrictive, were at best counsels of perfection, indications rather of a purpose than of an achievement, and they were often not even that. Frequently the Tudors regarded them simply as an opportunity to confer special favors or to secure additional revenue by granting dispensations in particular cases. This was notably true of laws regulating trade. For example, there had long

been laws on the statute-books prohibiting the
export of unfinished cloth in the interests of the
English finishing trades, yet as a matter of fact
a large export trade in unfinished cloth by special
license continued throughout the sixteenth century. The same thing was true of the navigation
laws. Henry VII was not the first English king
to promote legislation favorable to English carriers. The law passed in the first year of his reign
restricting the import of wine and woad from
western France to English bottoms was not a new
departure. More than a century previously
Richard II had limited all trade with England
to English ships. Nor was Henry's law consistently
enforced. He was an opportunist in this as in all
else. Other things being equal he preferred to
favor English traders and English ships as over
against foreign traders and foreign ships. But other
things were far from equal. The foreign carrier
and the foreign merchant were, and long remained, indispensable to English export trade and
neither Henry nor his successors were so wedded
to the interests of the English merchant that they
were prepared to jeopardize the larger interests
of the English export industries. We shall note as
the sixteenth century progresses the gradual de-
cline of the foreign carrier and the steady progress

of the English one, but the process was much slower and much less premeditated than has commonly been assumed. Under the early Tudors the German merchants of the Hansa, who were the most important of the foreign carriers, enjoyed a preferential tariff rate even as against English shippers, and in 1550 their exports of English cloth were double what they had been in 1500. It is to be noted that Henry VII took steps to break their monopoly in the Iceland trade and in the Baltic trade, but it was not until the reign of Elizabeth that they suffered to any marked degree from royal opposition. They were, of course, unpopular with London apprentices; on the other hand their wine shop in the Steelyard was a favorite resort for London gallants.

The Venetians, at the accession of Henry VII, virtually monopolized English trade in the Mediterranean, bringing in wine, sugar, currants and eastern luxuries, taking out wool and cloth. They shared the unpopularity of all foreigners with this added that as caterers to the tastes of the rich they were currently regarded as a menace to English morals. On the whole they were more dependent upon English wool than England was upon their commodities. This gave Henry the whip-hand and when the Venetian senate attempted to discriminate against English merchants in the Mediterranean he retaliated by establishing a staple for English wool at Pisa and confining the English Mediterranean wool trade to English ships. In consequence the Venetians finally had to yield. But apart from this incident Venetian traders were favored by the king and did not suffer any diminution of their privileges until the reign of his son. They continued to control most of the traffic between England and the Mediterranean until late in the reign of Elizabeth.

As for the English traders, Henry found them at his accession more or less loosely organized into two great bodies, the Staplers and the Merchant Adventurers. They were commonly called companies, but the term was used in its original sense of fellowships. The character of these organizations was that of the medieval trade-guild, not of the modern joint stock company. They were groups of professional merchants, trading as individuals with their own capital and at their own risk, but subject to certain regulations allowed by royal charter and imposed by the group as a whole upon its members. Of the two, the Staplers were the older. They monopolized the English export trade in wool. They were subject to rather strict governmental oversight, chiefly because of the importance of the export duties on wool to the royal exchequer. A regular channel for the foreign out-flow of wool was in fact defined with designated ports of export in England and a final port at Calais through which virtually all wool out of England in English bottoms had to be cleared.

So long as raw wool remained the chief com-modity of English export the Staplers were easily the most important group of English traders. But long before Henry's accession the export of cloth had developed to imposing dimensions. A good deal of it was carried out as we have seen by the German and the Italian traders. But a good deal of it was carried out also by English adventurers. Probably many of these operated as individuals on their own initiative. Many of them operated also in groups. It is not important in this connec-tion to attempt to unravel their obscure earlier history. Obviously in days when there was no elaborate consular service for the protection of English trading interests individual trading was a very rash adventure and those merchants who operated in large groups were in a much stronger position. Under these circumstances it is not sur-prising to discover that that particular group of Merchant Adventurers who were associated with London had come, by the end of the fifteenth century, to occupy a dominant position. They claimed in fact a monopoly of the English cloth trade with that part of Europe which lay between the river Somme in France and the Cattegat and attempted to enforce this monopoly by imposing a fee of £20 upon all merchants not of their fellowship who traded in that region. The situation had taken this form when it came to the attention of Henry VII. His action, or rather the action of his parliament in 1497, reveals his attitude. He said that the charge of £20 was too high and he fixed it at 20 marks. But by so doing he virtually conceded the right of the London adventurers to control the trade. A little later in his reign he granted them a charter and from that time forward the principle was clearly established that the English cloth trade with the great marts of the Low Countries and western Germany was, so far as English traders were concerned, the monopoly of the incorporated Merchant Adventurers. With the steady increase of the export of cloth this company assumed increasingly large proportions. It was easily the most important group of English merchants in Tudor England—important enough financially to be of material assistance to the crown when it needed to raise loans on short notice.

In the main Henry's interest in the development of trade was confined to trade in the conventional channels. His reign coincided exactly in point of time with the great adventures of Columbus, Vasco da Gama and the rest, but we discover nothing in Henry comparable, for example, to the long and persistent efforts of Prince Henry of Portugal to open up new regions of trade. For that matter, we discover little or nothing in the way of maritime enterprise among the English at large. The great English seafarers of the Tudor period were none of them yet born. Practically without exception the early discoverers were of the south, most of them Italians, a few Portuguese. Some exception should perhaps be made in favor of the sailors of Bristol, but the records of their deeds are too scanty to reveal more than an enterprising spirit. They apparently never got anywhere if they did put forth. It is, however, certain that Henry and the English had some share in the early voyages of discovery, if not as navigators at any rate as patrons and investors. There is good reason to believe that Christopher Columbus appealed to the English king for assistance in financing his great voyage of discovery and that Henry was not indisposed to help him, though he postponed his decision so long that Isabella of Spain forestalled him. It is certain that he did fit out a ship for John Cabot's first western voyage in 1497 and gave him a royal patent to any lands he might discover. He made possible a second Cabot voyage in the following year, and a few years later granted a charter of trade and colonization to a group of Bristol merchants. So far as can be gathered from the scanty evidence on the subject the English efforts were directed towards the region around the Gulf of Saint Lawrence. Probably the desire to avoid conflict with Spain prevented the exploitation of the obviously more promising regions of America farther south. In any case nothing came of it at all except an English claim to the coast of North America which was made much later when the economic possibilities of what is now the United States became more apparent. The disposition is to make more of Henry's interest in maritime discovery than the facts warrant. He granted a few charters, he may have fitted out one small ship. He certainly pensioned John Cabot and his private accounts show that he distributed a few pounds here and there to returning voyagers who brought him parrots and wildcats. But it is probable that his total expenditure was considerably less than £500. England at large, if we are to judge by the almost

complete absence of contemporary comment, ignored the whole enterprise.

Henry's interest in England's foreign trade,
whether in the old world or in the new, was a very
important factor in the determination of his foreign policy. His foreign relations were, like every
other problem he had to face, a strange blending
of elements old and new. Though he was singularly free from the prepossessions of his times, no
one knew better than he the world in which he
lived and the prime necessity of never losing contact with it. Once again he was nothing if not an
opportunist. He never let his opinion of what was
desirable blind him for a minute to what was possible. So far as his foreign problem was concerned
he found himself in an England which regarded
France and Scotland as the traditional enemies,
the Low Countries as ancient and economically
desirable friends and the rest of Europe with
complete indifference. England, despite the fact
that nothing more was left of her ancient posses-
sions in France than the town of Calais, still considered a large part of France as rightfully hers.
Henry, with the complete approval of his subjects,
still called himself king of France and still quartered the French lilies upon the royal shield.
Those who had been the friends of England in

her Hundred Years War with France still, in the popular English mind, remained friends, those who had been enemies, still enemies. More than that the English were predisposed to favor any power in Europe hostile to France. An alliance with the Habsburgs in Germany or with the new Spanish kingdom, but just completed by the marriage of Ferdinand of Aragon with Isabella of Castile, or with Brittany, the last of the French provinces to resist annexation to France, could expect popular support. It will not be too much to say that hostility to France constituted the most stable element in English foreign relations for the greater part of the Tudor period. Occasionally the Tudors ventured to deviate from that course, but they did it in the face of popular disapproval. It was not until the days of Elizabeth that the English as a nation abandoned their antipathy towards France because of the more immediate danger from Spain.

Henry VII for his part was disposed to regard this Gallophobia as a creed outworn. He certainly was not prepared to deplete the resources of England by expensive attempts to recover her old French empire. The king of France had, moreover, befriended him in the days of his exile. Nevertheless, if we leave out of account the endemic conflict on the Scottish border the only war in which Henry engaged was with France. He was drawn into it by an appeal for aid from Brittany. Probably he foresaw that Brittany's absorption by France was inevitable, but he dared not stand by and witness the extinction of an old ally by an old enemy without lending a hand. It might be wise but to fifteenth-century eyes it looked pusillanimous and Henry had his reputation to consider, not only in England but also in Europe at large. The war itself was more or less of a farce and Henry was glad to end it in 1492 on terms which gave him a considerable sum of money and a favorable commercial treaty.

In so far as he committed himself to a policy hostile to France he committed himself also to a policy of alliance with the enemies of France; namely, with Spain and the Holy Roman Empire. Ferdinand of Aragon, who directed the policy of the Spanish kingdoms, was, like Henry, an arch opportunist. For the moment he was hostile to France because he coveted the border provinces of Cerdagne and Roussillon and because he saw in the French ambitions in Italy a menace to his own position there. He was not, however, prepared to put strong armies in the field, being still deep in the business of conquering the Moorish kingdom in Grenada. Ferdinand's idea was to get other princes to pull his French chestnuts out of the fire and he was quite prepared to consider at least a temporary alliance with Henry to that end. Henry for his part was not interested in other people's chestnuts unless for a substantial *quid pro quo*. Ferdinand had a marriageable daughter, Katherine, and Henry a marriageable son, in fact two marriageable sons, Arthur and Henry. A marriage alliance with the proudest house in Europe would go far to strengthen his own position abroad and to secure the support of Spain against pretenders to the English throne. So the issue was joined and Ferdinand and Henry each maneuvered to get the better of the other. It is to be noted, as a measure of Henry's developing position in European politics, that whereas at the outset he was seeking a Spanish alliance, in the end the Spaniards were fearful that they would lose him. Eventually Ferdinand got his provinces and Henry his marriage alliance. What was more to Henry's immediate purpose he established his reputation as one of the wisest old foxes in Christendom.

With the empire Henry's relations were much more complicated. Maximilian, the emperor, by marrying the heiress of Charles the Bold of Burgundy had added to his Habsburg dominions in

Germany all that was left of the old Burgundian duchy, including the Low Countries. He thus joined to his own causes for quarrel the Burgundian hostility to France. At the same time he acquired with the Low Countries a traditional commercial alliance with England. If this had been all it would have been quite enough to have justified an alliance between Maximilian and Henry against France. But it was not all. Charles the Bold had married Margaret of York and in the War of the Roses had been the strongest ally of the Yorkists overseas. Charles to be sure was dead but Margaret survived and still held court as dowager duchess in the Low Countries. She regarded Henry VII as a Lancastrian usurper and she bore him besides a private grudge because he had confiscated a large part of her dowry at his accession. What influence she could exert over the policy of her son-in-law Maximilian, and she was a resolute woman, was directed steadily against Henry. She was not anti-English, she was anti-Lancastrian and her plan of action was to depose Henry and to place some one of the various Yorkist pretenders in his place. She supported Lambert Simnel, she supported much more vigorously Perkin Warbeck. It was largely due to her machinations that Warbeck was received and recognized in virtually every court in Europe.

It is easy, with foreknowledge of the outcome, to dismiss these pretenders as transparent frauds, but we can safely assume that a man of Henry's sanity and poise would not have been so distracted by them as he was if they had not been a real menace to his security. They were certainly a factor of first-rate importance in his relations with the Empire and with the Low Countries. The countenance and promises of support which Henry gave to Maximilian's projects against France were evidently prompted in large part by his desire to drive the pretenders from their European bases of support.

They were prompted also by a desire to secure for England a favorable commercial treaty with the Low Countries. In his diplomatic maneuvers with that wild dreamer Maximilian, Henry had the great advantage that his objectives were limited, definite and concrete. He might talk of joining forces to prevent French domination of Italy; he might even encourage Maximilian to hope for English assistance in a crusade against the Turks; but all he really wanted was peace, security and good business. And all these he got. One by one Maximilian broke with the various Yorkist pretenders. The last of them was brought over to England by his son's own messengers in 1506. Even Margaret of Burgundy before she died was obliged to apologize to Henry for her factiousness. The commercial treaties were a more tedious business. The so-called Intercursus Magnus of 1496 established free commercial intercourse between England and the Netherlands, but it was broken a few months after it was signed and though it was signed again in 1499 it was broken again in 1504—this time so completely broken that all trading stopped and Henry transferred the English cloth market from Antwerp to Calais. Two years later a storm in the English Channel cast Maximilian's young son Philip upon the English coast. Henry, in a rather unchivalrous fashion, seized the opportunity to negotiate a new treaty, which, in addition to all earlier concessions, exempted English traders from many vexatious local tolls and even gave them the right to sell English cloth at retail in all the Netherlands except Flanders. Philip repudiated the engagement when he was safely out of England again and Henry, realizing that he had pressed his advantage too far, consented to its modification the following year. Even so, he gained his point. At his death the English cloth trade was once again securely established in the Low Countries where it was to grow steadily for the next fifty years.

One other element in Henry's foreign policy remains to be considered: that of his neighbor in the north—Scotland. There was and had been very little that was neighborly about the relations of England and Scotland. They were in fact inveterate enemies and the borderland between them was the seat of almost uninterrupted warfare. The Scots feared absorption by England considerably more than they feared either God or the devil, and though English kings during the whole of the fifteenth century had been too busily engaged elsewhere to attempt to recover the sovereignty over the north which Edward II had lost at Bannockburn, the Scots always expected them and were always ready to join forces with their enemies. Even when no war was afoot Scottish borderers were never averse from a cattle raid in English territory. During England's Hundred Years War with France the Scots were almost always allies of the French. If there was any stability at all in the policy of their disordered country it resided in an inveterate friendship for France and an inveterate hostility to England.

Henry VII himself had no quarrel with Scotland and with some minor interruptions managed to keep the peace in the north for ten years. But the appeal for help from Perkin Warbeck was too tempting for James IV of Scotland to resist. In 1495 he invited Warbeck to Scotland, granted him a liberal pension and gave him a noble wife. More than that, he undertook a war against Henry in Warbeck's behalf. James led a Scottish army into England in 1495 and again in 1497, hoping to arouse rebellion there in Warbeck's favor. But each time he led his army back again with no more decisive results than a few burning English villages. All this was in the old tradition but James lacked the means and Henry the inclination to continue it indefinitely. A truce was arranged in 1497. The year before Henry had proposed a marriage between Margaret, his elder daughter, and the Scottish king. James of Scotland proved favorably inclined but it was not until 1502 that a marriage treaty was finally arranged. Henry scouted the idea that such a match might lead to the subjection of England. "The greater," he said, "would draw the less."

So far as Henry's own problem was concerned Margaret's marriage accomplished its purpose and established peace in the north for the remainder of his reign. It led ultimately to the union of England and Scotland under James the First and Sixth about a century later. But so far as Tudor England was concerned it provided no more than a very short interlude in the long story of Anglo-Scottish hostility. We shall see presently that Henry's son and his grandchildren were as much plagued by the Scottish problem as any English rulers ever had been.

Henry, like most of his contemporaries, had a childlike faith in the efficacy of marriage as a bond of political union. It may fairly be observed that every match which he arranged had momentous consequences though these consequences were far other than he designed. Out of Margaret's unhappy match sprang the union of England and Scotland, out of his son Henry's marriage with Katherine of Aragon the break of England from the Roman church. Henry had arranged his own marriage with Elizabeth of York for political reasons, though it proved to be a happy match. Elizabeth was a beautiful and a very lovable woman and Henry's relations with her reveal dim glimpses of quite a different man from the cold calculating statesman of his public life. She died in 1503. In spite of Henry's genuine affection for her it was not more than a year after her death before he was contemplating a second marriage. It is not at all clear what his political objectives were in his various excursions in search of another wife but the search itself was characteristic. Henry realized the diplomatic advantage accruing from his unmarried state just as his granddaughter Elizabeth did later and he utilized it for all that it might be worth. We need not follow him in his later philanderings nor assume that they had any emotional significance so far as he was personally concerned. His nice curiosity about the physical attributes of the various ladies he had under consideration disclose the fact that he was not entirely indifferent to such matters. But there is a certain unreality about all of Henry's foreign relations during the last five or six years of his life. His major problems had been solved. He had arranged good marriages for all except the youngest of his children, Mary, who was a mere baby. Arthur, his first-born, the bridegroom of Katherine of Aragon, died young, but Henry, his second son, was promptly affianced to his brother's widow. Margaret, his elder daughter, was married to James of Scotland. The pretenders had all been disposed of one way or another. Favorable commercial treaties had been arranged with France, with Spain and with the Low Countries. Henry's prestige was firmly established in Europe. He had attained all his chief objectives. He cherished no imperial designs; he was not ambitious for military glory. The latter end of his life was devoted to the task of consolidating his position. That probably explains why he became thrifty to the point of miserliness. Like a prudent business man he was building up his reserves.

Henry died in 1509 and was laid away in the beautiful chapel he had added to Westminster Abbey. It is customary to inquire whether or not he was a great king but the question is an idle one until we have defined greatness. He was not a splendid king, he was pretty clearly not a well-beloved king, but he was without doubt a very successful king. "What he minded that he compassed." Perhaps he was successful precisely for the reason that his objective was limited. His reach never exceeded his grasp. He saw his problem clearly, defined it in terms which admitted of a solution and then solved it. His first business was to establish his dynasty after thirty years of dynastic struggle. He established his dynasty. His second problem was to make England secure within and without under a strong monarchy. That also he did. His final problem perhaps was to set up a reserve against possible contingencies and he left behind him the richest treasury in Christendom.

In the process he imposed upon England a new

conception of royal leadership which was to secure for his house the enthusiastic loyalty of his subjects until nearly a century later the last of his line was laid beside him in Westminster Abbey. But somehow his performance never caught the popular imagination. It was all so eminently sane and intelligent—no trumpets, no drum beats, no snow-white plumes, no palpable trophies. One of the greatest of modern historians finds his reign dull. Laying foundations can be dull work especially when, as in Henry's case, it is merely a business of setting stone upon stone with no vision of the splendid edifice which is to mount above them.

HENRY VIII

CHAPTER II

HENRY VIII

ENRY VII was given a magnificent burial but there were few tears to grace his obsequies. Bosworth Field was a long way off. Englishmen had almost forgotten the Wars of the Roses and had come to accept the peaceful, prosperous and orderly England that the wise old king had made for them as in the natural course of things. What they remembered was his cautious and suspicious personality, his cold eye, his grasping hand. He had given them security but it was of a dismal and forbidding sort, the security of a man within prison walls. What they wanted now was air, color, sunlight—a merrie England.

And the new king bade fair to give it to them. Young Henry VIII was indeed all that a king should be. Just short of eighteen years of age, he appeared to have every grace of mind and body. The foreign ambassadors at the English court vied with one another in the description of his talents. He spoke Latin, French, Spanish and some little

[43]

Italian; he played with skill both the lute and the harpsicord and already had revealed evidence of very considerable gifts as a composer. He was an admirable horseman, a capital shot with the long bow, a fine tennis player. One admirer wrote, "It is the prettiest thing in the world to see him play, his fair skin glowing through a shirt of finest texture." The Venetian ambassador declared him to be the handsomest sovereign in Christendom. No wonder if England was glad to forget its cold, bald and almost toothless mentor late deceased in the presence of this paragon.

Young Henry, for his part, was too much preoccupied with the joy of living to give more than a perfunctory regard to the affairs of state. In accordance with his father's wishes he proceeded with almost indecent haste to complete the arrangements for his marriage to Katherine of Aragon. Barely a month after Henry VII's death the ceremony was performed, to be followed by a week of merrymaking. The shadow of a doubt about the legitimacy of the match within the degrees prohibited by canon law was dissipated by a papal dispensation—at least for the time being. The merrymaking was very much to the popular taste. So was the condemnation of Empson and Dudley, the late, monarch's extortionate ministers. They were both sent to the block on a trumped-up charge of treason while the people applauded. They applauded still louder when the fines which had been imposed but not yet collected were canceled by royal grace. But these measures taken, Henry reverted to his music, his hunting and his tennis matches, well content to leave the details of administration to the wise old councilors his father had bequeathed to him. He was after all, despite his precocity, little more than a boy.

No one saluted Henry VIII's accession with more enthusiasm than the small group of scholars and men of letters who had gathered together in England at the close of the fifteenth century. One of them wrote in Latin to his friend Erasmus: "The heavens laugh, the earth exults, all things are full of milk, of honey and of nectar. Avarice is expelled the country, liberality scatters wealth with a bounteous hand. The king does not desire gold or gems or precious metals, but virtue, glory, immortality." The utterance is no doubt extravagant and reveals a writer more concerned about his fine latinity than about exact precision of statement, but it expresses the hopes and expectations of men who were the harbingers in England of a movement of fundamental importance to English life and thought.

This movement we call the renaissance. In its essence it was a changed attitude of mind towards man and his environment, substituting for the medieval conception of man as a miserable sinner striving against the world and the flesh, man as an interesting and beautiful creature in a beautiful and interesting world. Burkhardt defines it as the discovery of the world and of man. It manifested itself in every department of human activity, in thought and in action, in pleasure and in business, in all the arts and in all the sciences. We have it to thank for the paintings of Leonardo and Raphael, the sculpture of Angelo, the statescraft of Machiavelli, the scholarship of Erasmus, the philosophy of Bruno, the celestial revelations of Copernicus, the terrestrial revelations of Columbus and Vasco da Gama, to mention only those of the first magnitude in a whole galaxy of stars. It was in short the impulse which set in motion the whole modern world.

The renaissance is often defined in terms of a reversion to classical culture, but the definition is misleading. Men turned to ancient models, not so much out of any reverence for the Greeks and the Romans *per se* as because they found in the classics the most satisfactory expression of what they themselves were trying to express. It is customary

also to speak of the renaissance as Italian. It was
Italian in this, that it revealed itself first in Italy
and in some departments of human culture, notably in the fine arts, found its most complete expression in Italy. But the impulse was universal
and those who felt it merely turned to Italy as
they turned to the classics for further inspiration
and guidance. The result was that Italy did have
a very profound influence on the direction of
European culture, particularly in the sixteenth
century when the impulse was still fresh and when
other nations had not yet found their own best
media of expression. Italy in short became the
fashion, and many Italian plants were accordingly
transplanted to soils not at all congenial to them.
This is always so and it always in time produces
a reaction; hence the denunciation of the Italianate
Englishman later in the century. But when Henry
VIII came to the throne, Italy was the Mecca of
progressively-minded Englishmen in every walk
of life. The scholars went there to perfect their
scholarship, the artists their painting and sculpture
and architecture, the doctors their medicine, the
lawyers their law. The merchant and the banker
found there the best school of commerce and
finance, the budding statesman the clearest exposi-
tion of the new statescraft and the new diplomacy.

Even the scriveners looked to Italy for new models of handwriting, even the dandies aped the Italian fashions in dress and manners.

The Englishman did not always prove himself to be an apt pupil. He made almost no progress in the fine arts. There was little native painting and no native sculpture worth mentioning in sixteenth century England and though there were some glorious architectural achievements such as Henry VII's chapel at Westminster, King's College Chapel at Cambridge and the Magdalen Tower at Oxford, these all belong to the sunset splendors of English gothic and reveal little or nothing of the new spirit. Outside of a few pretentious private dwellings English architecture proceeded along traditional lines until well into the seventeenth century. In *belles-lettres* the influence of the Italian renaissance was more apparent, but in Henry VIII's time this hardly extended beyond the purlieus of the court circle and found its most manifest expression in the experiments of two courtiers, Sir Thomas Wyatt and the Earl of Surrey, with the Italian sonnet form. Its broader literary influences revealed themselves later.

So far as the first half of the sixteenth century is in question, the impulse of the renaissance is most clearly revealed in England by a small group of scholars who are commonly known as the Oxford reformers. Of these the outstanding figures were John Colet and Thomas More, but Thomas Linacre and William Grocyn were conspicuous and, during the time of his sojourn in England, the great Dutch scholar, Desiderius Erasmus of Rotterdam. Linacre's fame is associated with the advancement of medical knowledge, though it was as a Greek scholar that he attracted the attention of his contemporaries. The rest were all enthusiastic students of Greek and of the classical learning in general. But none of them stopped at mere scholarship. One and all, and in particular Colet, More and Erasmus, directed the resources of their learning to the reform of men and of methods. They were chiefly concerned about the church, intent to deliver her from the webs of medieval scholasticism and to establish the essentials of Christianity upon an exact understanding of Holy Writ. They were equally zealous in their attacks upon the ecclesiastical abuses of the times. So far they went *pari passu* with the Protestant reformers who followed them. But they never contemplated a breach with the Roman church and when the test came later those who survived, notably More and Erasmus, stood out manfully in defense of the old dispensation. But their significance in the development of England is rather as humanists than as churchmen. Their zeal for learning, their method of careful and critical inquiry, above all their passion to apply their talents to the enlightenment and improvement of their fellows, mattered most. It was characteristic of Thomas More, the greatest and best of them, that though he wavered for a time between a political and an ecclesiastical career he decided in the end in favor of politics and came ultimately to occupy the highest judicial position in the gift of the crown. And it was not inappropriate, though More probably never intended it, that his most important contribution to the history of human thought should be his description of an ideal commonwealth—Utopia.

It is one of the paradoxes of modern history that in England and in the north of Europe in general so much of the intellectual stimulus of the renaissance movement should have been diverted to religious thinking. For the renaissance was quite definitely secular in spirit and to a considerable extent represented a reaction against the religious prepossessions of the age which had preceded it. But so it was, and, whether for better or for worse, most of the best minds in sixteenth century England became immersed in theological disputes and many of the bravest spirits were sacrificed upon the altar of this church or that. Even Henry VIII himself was guilty of a theological pamphlet and won the title of Defender of the Faith by a published attack upon Martin Luther. In the main, however, the Tudors were not theologically-minded and they steadily discouraged, even when they did not positively prohibit, religious controversy. In consequence, though none of them was remarkable as a patron of the arts, they provided the atmosphere in which the arts could flourish. Without them the finest fruits of the English genius in the sixteenth century might have been trampled under foot in the battle of contending creeds. Christopher Marlowe might have been burned at the stake as an atheist and William Shakespeare might have suffered the fate of Sir Thomas More.

There was one aspect of the renaissance in which the Tudors were profoundly interested and that was its politics. The development of a centralized state under a strong king was generally characteristic, as we have seen, of western Europe at the close of the fifteenth century. It took place at the expense of feudalism and necessitated the selection of an administrative personnel untainted by

feudal conceptions of government. The kings of
the new dispensation, like the artists, found their
pattern in the classical world and their counselors
among those who had been trained in the Roman
conception of monarchy. It was no accident that
the growth of royal absolutism was accompanied
by a revival of the study of Roman law. And here
again Italy became the school for the whole west
and Bologna, and later Padua, the schoolrooms.
Through this channel Italy did much to weaken,
not only the feudal conception of monarchy, but
the whole feudal law. In France, in Italy and in
Spain the national law, already basically Roman,
became almost completely Romanized. In the
Holy Roman Empire the Germanic law was definitely set aside in favor of the Corpus Juris. English jurisprudence put up a stiffer resistance to
this alien influence. It had its text-books, its case-
books, its commentators—most important of all it
had its law schools strongly entrenched in the inns
of court. Nevertheless it had to fight for its life
in the first half of the sixteenth century. In the end
it triumphed, but not before the Roman law had
left its marks upon almost every branch of the
English law, notably upon those which impinged
upon international relations, like the admiralty
law, and those which dealt with the whole field

of equitable jurisdiction, to wit, the courts of chancery. We are concerned, however, primarily with the law as it regulated the relations of individuals to the state. From this point of view the Roman imperial code was undoubtedly attractive to the monarchs of the new dispensation as it was to their civilian advisers. Its influence in England was greater in determining the political and legal attitudes of Tudor governors than in any concrete modification of the national law *per se*. The effects of this influence are apparent upon the organs of Tudor government, notably upon the Privy Council and the prerogative courts. Probably it had much to do also with shaping the theories of kingship as they appear in the English political writings of the times. Henry VIII's break from Rome called forth, for example, vigorous exponents of the royal supremacy as opposed to the papal supremacy in matters ecclesiastical. It is significant that the two outstanding champions of the king's position, Stephen Gardiner and Christopher Saint German, were both of them steeped in the principles of the Roman law.

While the revival of interest in Roman jurisprudence was breeding up a school of absolutists among the law students, a practical politician in Italy was erecting very much the same political gospel upon the grounds of mere expediency. Niccolo Machiavelli was not well thought of in sixteenth century England. In the popular mind his name became synonymous "for whatever was most loathsome in statecraft and indeed in human nature at large." And that opinion of him overshadows the importance of his contribution to political theory even to the present day. His influence, nevertheless, was profound, not so much perhaps because of the originality of his views as because he gave expression to a practical as opposed to a theoretical approach to political problems, an inductive as opposed to a deductive method of considering them, which marched with the tendencies of the times. After a careful survey of actual conditions in Italy Machiavelli reached the conclusion that royal despotism was the most efficient form of government and that abstract considerations of moral rectitude had often to give way to considerations of practical expediency. There is very little evidence that his writings were generally known in England before the middle of the century. What we may call, for want of a better name, Machiavellian influences in Tudor politics came rather from Italy direct through the personal contact of prominent English statesmen with the Italian political atmosphere. All the great

Tudor statesmen, with the exception of Wolsey and the elder Cecil, were men of Italian training. Thomas Cromwell was completely saturated with Machiavelli's political philosophy; Francis Walsingham, Elizabeth's right-hand man, was denounced by King James of Scotland as "a very Machiavel." Henry VIII himself has been described as Machiavelli's prince in action.

How much of Tudor absolutism we should ascribe to the influence of the Roman law and how much to Italian inspiration it is not possible and hardly necessary to say. The great Tudors were practical politicians by nature and very probably would have reached the position they did without the assistance of either Rome or Florence. They avoided theorizing and justified their course of action simply by the results they achieved. Nevertheless the trend of contemporary political thinking was distinctly favorable to their purposes. It supplied a harmonious stage setting for their performance, a formal justification of their policy, and most important perhaps of all a well-disciplined personnel out of which they could build an efficient political machine.

During the first twenty years of Henry VIII's reign the dominating figure in English public life was Thomas Wolsey. His career is typical of

Tudor statesmen, though he rose higher than any of the rest of them. He had no pedigree. There is no tracing of his line behind his father and we know nothing of his father except that he was of Ipswich and a grazier. His course of advancement was through the church, the most promising course for a man of energy, brains and no connections. Henry VII had recognized his ability and used him. He entered Henry VIII's council in 1511, being then about forty years of age and some twenty years older than the king. After that his rise was phenomenally rapid. In three years he had climbed to be Archbishop of York, the second place in the English church, and the year after that to be lord chancellor, the highest position in the gift of the crown. He was my lord cardinal in 1515 and three years later papal legate from the side of (*à latere*) a pope he had never seen and from Rome which he had never visited. The secret of his progress was pure competency. He worked harder, more intelligently and more efficiently than any other man in public service. He relieved the king of all the details of government. Indeed he appeared to overshadow Henry himself. But none knew better than Wolsey that all that he had he owed to the royal favor and that the hand which had been strong to raise him was equally strong to pull him down. It was characteristic of Henry as it was of his father and his daughter that he knew how to select competent servants.

Wolsey became proud and arrogant to an intolerable degree. Deferential and subservient to his master, he was careless of all the rest of England besides. He successively antagonized the nobility by his attacks upon their special privileges, the commons by his attack upon their purse and the clergy by his encroachments upon their liberties. In short he set up his rest upon the royal favor and when that failed him he fell like Lucifer, never to hope again.

The period of his domination is the period in which England played its most active part in foreign affairs. With one exception all the wars which Henry VIII fought were organized and directed by the great cardinal. He not only drew England very definitely into the concert of the European powers but made a very conspicuous plan for her there. The neighbors he had to deal with were France, Spain, Burgundy and the Empire, with France as the hereditary foe and Burgundy the hereditary friend. Scotland, so far as her relations with England were in question, was little more than an apanage of France. Spain was tied fairly close by marriage bonds with no fundamental points at issue, such as religion and America were to become later. Katherine of Aragon, during the first ten years of her husband's reign, did much to promote good will between her native country and her adopted one. Burgundy meant for England the Low Countries and the Low Countries meant the best market for English wool and English cloth. As for the Empire, it hardly mattered except that it could generally be counted upon to oppose France. A little later when Spain and Burgundy and the Empire were all gathered together under Charles V the natural allies of England marched under the same banner. By 1520 Europe was really divided into two camps and the dominating factor in international affairs was the rivalry of Valois and Habsburg. This leaves out of account the Turk, a dark and steadily enlarging cloud to the southeast with which England was little concerned, and the papacy, which one distinguished historian at least believes to have been the most important factor in Wolsey's calculations. It is certain that Wolsey was more Habsburg than he was Valois and indubitable that his fighting was all against France and against her Scottish ally. But there are no Crécys and Agincourts in English annals at this time though royal panegyrists made much of Henry's victory at Therouanne and his capture of Tournai. The most important single battle was in the north on Flodden Field where the Scottish king was killed and most of his chivalry with him. Not much that was constructive came from any of these engagements unless it was a demonstration of what was already clear, that Scotland was no match for England even when her king was overseas, and that anything like an English reconquest of her old French dominions was quite out of the question. Certainly Wolsey raised England to a position in Europe which she had not occupied since the death of Henry V. The evidence tends to show that he played steadily on the side of the pope and considered it essential to keep England and the papacy in harmony. Possibly he recognized that England by reason of her insular position and the papacy by reason of its common interest in all Christendom were the two elements in the whole international situation best fitted to maintain the equilibrium between contending forces. Possibly he was prompted chiefly by his own personal aspirations for the papal crown. In any case he held his course successfully so long as he could drive pope and king in double harness. When the famous divorce case tore them apart, he fell between them.

Preoccupation with Wolsey's brilliant diplomacy has tended to obscure his very considerable achievements in domestic affairs. As lord chancellor he did much to stimulate the whole development of equitable jurisdiction. He, more than anyone else, shaped the Court of Star Chamber into the powerful instrument by which virtually the last vestiges of feudal disorder and feudal privilege were swept away. As papal legate he made himself supreme in the English church, ruthlessly thrusting aside the contending claims of bishops, archbishops and convocation. In fact he did much by his arbitrary and despotic exercise of papal power to discredit the papacy in the eyes of English churchmen and so eased the way for the breach with Rome which he himself, had he lived, would have been the last to approve. There can be no doubt that he exploited the resources of the church for his own purposes, diverted the most profitable cases within her jurisdiction to his own courts and contemptuously ignored her rights of election. He was quite intolerant of anything like democratic control.

This was equally true of his dealings with parliament. He shared Henry VII's antipathy to parliament, regarded it at best as a necessary evil, called it as little as he might and undertook to browbeat it when he did call it. And so it was that having antagonized the nobility in Star Chamber and the church with his legatine commissions he defied fate and alienated as well the mainstay of the Tudor monarchy, the bourgeoisie.

Wolsey's greatness lay in his competency, his folly in his arrogance and pride, his fundamental mistake in his preoccupation rather with foreign than with domestic problems. No doubt he was a splendid figure in his scarlet robes and no doubt he won for England a splendid place in the councils of Europe. But England did not want cardinals nor did she want diplomatic prestige. What she did want Henry VII had in part discerned and Henry VIII was presently to discover. It was an England free from foreign entanglements, safe behind her sea-walls against the envy of less happier lands; peace, good order and good business. And so Wolsey's magnificent adventure contributed little or nothing except to provoke a reaction against all that he stood for and to hasten progress in the direction opposite to that in which he had marched.

The cause of his undoing was the famous divorce case. Henry VIII concluded sometime in the late 1520's that he was not legally married to his wife Katherine of Aragon and decided to secure the annulment of the marriage from the pope. The reasons for the decision were in part dynastic, in large measure personal. Of the six children born to Katherine only one, a daughter, had survived and after 1525 it was known that Katherine could bear no more children. Unless something were done about it, the succession, after the king's death, would inevitably devolve upon a woman, a broken reed for a young dynasty not yet secure upon the throne to lean upon. On these grounds Henry was justified in giving the matter serious consideration. There had been a canonical irregularity about his marriage to his brother's wife and although the pope had granted dispensation it was open to question as to whether even the pope could dispense with Holy Writ. The matter was plain enough in Leviticus (xx: 21): "And if a man shall take his brother's wife it is an unclean thing, he hath uncovered his brother's nakedness. They shall be childless." [1] And Henry was childless or nearly so. It looked a little like the judgment of God.

And then there was Anne Boleyn. She was not the first of Henry's love affairs but there was no doubt about the reality and intensity of his passion.

[1] Of course Deuteronomy xxv: 5 put quite a different complexion on the matter.

He wanted her as quickly as might be but she held him at arm's length—willing enough to be his wife but not to be his mistress. For something like five years she succeeded in holding him at arm's length, a remarkable performance, all things considered, and probably indicative that there was considerably more of cold calculation than of passion in Anne's attitude. Henry had every reason to expect that the pope would lend a favorable ear to his appeal for an annulment of his marriage—as much had been done both for his brother-in-law and for his sister on much shakier grounds. The appeal was accordingly made to Rome late in the year 1527. All might have been well, presumably would have been well, had the pope been a free agent. But he was at the time virtually a prisoner in the hands of the Emperor Charles V, and Charles V was Katherine of Aragon's nephew. So it was that the affair dragged on to interminable length, the pope fearing to alienate Henry by refusing his request or Charles by granting it. Wolsey worked hard to accomplish his master's purposes and succeeded in persuading the pope to send Cardinal Campeggio from Rome to join with him in passing judgment on the matter. But nothing came of it except an opportunity for Katherine to bear herself in truly queenly fashion. At the last

Campeggio adjourned the court without a decision and a little later the pope, acting under strong pressure from the emperor, revoked the case to Rome and cited Henry and his wife to appear before the Roman curia.

That was the end of any hope of immediate success from the policy which Wolsey had pursued feverishly for two years. He had not favored the divorce, it had upset all his diplomatic arrangements, but he had done his best to achieve it. And he had failed and that was the end of him. The story of his fall need not be retold. Death mercifully intervened to save him from the final humiliation.

As for Henry, he was more resolute than ever to proceed. His next step was to summon parliament. It assembled in November 1529 and was destined to remain in session seven years and "to carry out a series of changes more profound and widespread than any which had yet been accomplished in the annals of English legislation." There is evidence enough to show that the king interested himself in the elections and that the majority of the commons consisted of royal officials. Even so it was by no means servile and probably "roughly representative of an orthodox, priest-hating, crown-loving nation." The significant fact after all is that Henry should have turned to parliament. That in itself marks a definite break with Wolsey, indeed a definite break with the Tudor tradition up to that time. We have here the first expression of Henry VIII's definite acceptance and definite application of the principle of government by consent. It marks a turning point in English history, a turning point almost in the history of the western world, for had Wolsey's conception of government persisted England might have gone the way in which all the rest of Europe was to go, the way of absolute despotism. No matter if Henry packed his parliament or not, no matter if he completely dominated it. What mattered was that he made it an essential feature in his whole scheme of government. That was his great claim to distinction, perhaps his chief claim to be called great, and no preoccupation with his sex life and his multitudinous marriages ought to be allowed to obscure that fact. He was, as Professor Pollard has remarked, the greatest parliamentarian that ever sat on the English throne. That being so, it was well for the future of the world that he came just when he did, for at that precise moment the fate of popular government hung very precariously in the balance.

It may be that he got the idea from Thomas

Cromwell, a new man, who had been in Wolsey's service and who attracted Henry's. attention at about the time of Wolsey's fall. Certainly it was Cromwell who carried it out and who directed all the steps by which king and parliament together split England away from Rome, destroyed the monastic system and established a national church. Cromwell was a blacksmith's son who had climbed up the ladder from the very bottom by a rare combination of intelligence and efficiency coupled with a complete lack of moral scruples. He was the first great minister of the crown base-born and yet not a cleric. In his time he had been a trooper, a merchant and a money-lender on a large scale. Of religion he had little. What religion he had inclined him away from the old church and towards Lutheranism. His political philosophy was that of Machiavelli. The whole of his moral code was that the end justified the means. His chief objective was to establish the absolute power of the crown and he saw in the Roman church the great obstacle in the way. To break with Rome, that would take the divorce case out of papal hands and place it where it could not go wrong, that would divert to the crown all the powers and privileges and revenues of the pope in England. He offered

Henry power, wealth, Anne Boleyn. No wonder if Cromwell attracted the royal attention.

The various steps by which Henry broke away from Rome were taken one at a time, with a convenient pause between each step to see whether the pope was not yet ready to do the reasonable thing. Efforts were also made to apply pressure through France, to secure the independent support of the European universities, to resort to the time-honored device of an appeal to a council of the church. The whole procedure was worked out with consummate skill and with so much deliberation that five years intervened between the first step and the last. It was not by any means an easy business. In the autumn of 1529 Henry's international situation was worse than ever it had been; so was his financial situation. His people were more generally discontented than in any earlier part of his reign and they were generally sympathetic with his injured wife. And yet Henry managed it and managed also to carry England along with him. What he could count on was a strong popular feeling against papal interference in English affairs and a pretty strong hostility against the clergy on the grounds that they were neglecting their sacred duties and that they were gouging the commonality by taxes and charges of all sorts. It does

not appear that he could count on much open rebellion against the Roman Catholic faith and
dogma. Evidently he could not. He took particular care to emphasize his own orthodoxy just at
the time when he was striking his shrewdest blows
at pope and clergy. As a matter of fact there was
very little in the way of doctrinal deviation from
the old faith in his break from Rome, either in its
conception or in the realization. Pronounced Protestant influences came in later, after Henry had
been gathered to his fathers.

The attack began in the house of commons in
1529 and was directed against certain prevalent
abuses in the church, such as nonresidence of the
clergy, excessive fees collected at burials and excessive charges imposed at the probate of wills. It was
easy enough to invoke popular sentiment against
this sort of thing and it could have been done in
almost any parliament that had ever sat in England. It produced some anti-clerical legislation and
gave a distinct indication of the direction of the
royal purpose.

A year later, in December 1530, the pope still
remaining obdurate, Henry's attorney-general
lodged a charge against the whole body of the
English clergy on the grounds that by recognizing
the legatine authority of Wolsey they had broken

the old law of *praemunire*. The charge was pre-
posterous enough but it served its double purpose,
which was to extort money from the clergy and to
wring from them a declaration of submission. They
were allowed to purchase pardon by a substantial
grant to the king in convocation, on the grim condition that they would recognize Henry as supreme head of the church of England. This was
a hard morsel for them to swallow but they finally
contrived it with the modifying phrase, "so far as
the law of Christ allows." And that was the second
step, rather a long step, but so far as the pope was
concerned, it produced nothing. Henry turned then
once more to parliament and began a systematic
attack upon ecclesiastical legislation and jurisdiction with the net result that he forced the clergy
to submit all new constitutions, canons and ordi-
nances of the church for royal approval and all old
ones for royal ratification or revision. On top of
that he secured from parliament a bill to abolish
annates, the payment due to the pope from new
incumbents of ecclesiastical benefices. If it was to
be applied it would rob the pope of a large part of
his revenues from England. It was left to Henry's
discretion as to whether it should be applied or not.
Here the intention was unequivocal—no divorce,
no money. Nothing could be plainer.

Meanwhile Henry had definitely decided to take Anne to wife. During the year 1532 that fact was made pretty patent. Katherine was moved away from the court and the "lady" or the "concubine," as she was variously called, was lodged in her place. In October 1532, arrayed in the queen's jewels, she accompanied Henry on a visit to the French king at Calais. Sometime about then she capitulated. In January 1533 she was with child. It was essential, if not that her virtue should be saved, at least that her issue should be lawful. Since the pope proved more and more obdurate, notwithstanding the submission of the clergy and the restraint of annates, the divorce would have to be accomplished in England. By rare good luck the Archbishop of Canterbury died in August 1532 and Henry had a chance to appoint in his place an ecclesiastic quite sympathetic with his purposes. He pitched upon Thomas Cranmer, a man of keen intelligence and considerable learning, "destined in the prayer-book to exhibit his exquisite command of all the harmonies of the English language," a strong royalist, an equally strong anti-papalist, more definitely inclined towards doctrinal reformation than Henry perhaps would have wished, but quite discreet about the matter. The problem was to get his appointment regularly confirmed by the pope so that there could be no question of his competence when the time came to carry out the royal wishes. It was here that Henry was able to apply his discretionary power in the matter of the restraint of annates to advantage. And so Cranmer got the necessary papal bulls and was, with the usual formalities, inducted into his high office in the spring of 1533. All that was needed now was to refer the divorce question to an English ecclesiastical court under Cranmer's presidency—all except one thing. The right of appeal to Rome from the decision of that court must be cut off. A bill was accordingly pushed through parliament to that effect. In April 1533 Cranmer was ready to deal with the divorce question. The result was a foregone conclusion; in less than a fortnight Henry's marriage with Katherine of Aragon was declared null and void. Six weeks later Anne Boleyn, who had been secretly married to Henry in January, was crowned queen in Westminster Abbey. Three months after that she was delivered of a daughter—Elizabeth, the Good Queen Bess that was to be.

The final break with Rome was now inevitable. When parliament reassembled in January 1534 Cromwell was ready with the requisite legislation. All papal revenues from England, all appeals from English ecclesiastical courts to the Roman curia were cut off. Hereafter English archbishops and bishops were to be elected and inducted into their offices without reference to any alien power and no English cleric was to take any oath to the Roman pontiff. Later in the year the Act of Supremacy established the royal headship of the church without any limiting conditions—law of Christ or otherwise. The creed remained, the ritual remained, the ecclesiastical hierarchy remained, but with its head cut off, or rather with its head replaced. Where the pope had been, there now was Henry, at least so far as the juridical and political powers of the pope in England were in question. How much further the royal headship extended, how much it might do to determine personnel, reform canon law, amend ritual and purify doctrine was not quite so clear. Men were to dispute about these matters for a long time to come; men like the Puritans, who cared not a straw for the pope, were to wage bloody war about them.

The final act of defiance to Rome was the establishment of the English succession in the heirs of Henry and Anne. It came at just about the time that the pope was declaring the marriage of Henry and Katherine valid. And so the issue was clearly joined. Was the pope to say or was the king?

Henry would have no ambiguity about the matter. He insisted that all his subjects should take the oath to observe all the terms of the Act of Succession upon pain of misprision of treason. In such wise he proposed to winnow the wheat from the chaff.

The process of winnowing was difficult and cruel and some of the most gallant figures in English history paid the supreme penalty for their loyalty to the old faith. The Carthusian priors John Houghton, Augustine Webster and Robert Lawrence; the prior of Sion, Richard Reynolds, the vicar of Isleworth, John Hale—these names are written in letters of gold in the annals of Roman Catholicism. And so is the name of John Fisher, bishop of Rochester, and so above all is the name of Thomas More, one of the wisest and wittiest and noblest of men that ever trod the soil of England. And yet none of them died more bravely than thirteen miserable Dutch Anabaptists who were burned at the stake, though there were no crowns of martyrdom for them and even More would have approved. But such was the sixteenth century. No one really questioned the logic of persecution. What they questioned was Henry's program, not his methods of dealing with those who opposed it. As a matter of fact the English even in the sixteenth century were indifferent persecutors as measured by continental standards.

The martyrs were a glorious company but they were a small one. With remarkably few exceptions the whole body of the English clergy regular and secular accepted the royal decision. And the same was true of the laity. It must have been so, it could hardly have been otherwise, for Henry lacked the strength to impose his will upon a hostile people. He had no standing army, he had exhausted his father's financial reserves. His taxes were assessed and collected, his armed forces raised, his local justice and police controlled by the gentry in the country and their equivalent in the towns. Pretty clearly he could not have carried through his religious program if there had been general opposition—or even if there had not been general acquiescence. The best possible test of the popularity of Tudor legislation was its enforcement, for enforcement rested upon the good will of the freemen who made up the indictment juries and the good will of the justices of the peace who heard and determined.

Thomas Cromwell had promised his master among other things that he would make him the richest king in Christendom. That part of his program had only in part been realized. It was true

that the customary payments to the pope had been
diverted to the royal treasury, but a great deal
more than that was needed if the royal expectations
were not to be disappointed. That more Cromwell
undertook to provide from the property of the
church. In 1535 he had himself appointed vicar-
general of the king in all his ecclesiastical jurisdiction and directed to make a general visitation
of all the churches, monasteries and collegiate
bodies in the kingdom. What he had particularly
in mind were the monasteries and their wealth.
It was currently reported that they were a good
deal richer than they should be and generally
believed that they were no longer serving any
useful spiritual purpose. The usual stories were
told about the dissoluteness of their inhabitants.
There was reason enough that they should be
visited and promise enough that a visitation con-
ducted in the proper spirit would give abundant
grounds for wholesale confiscations. Cromwell's
commissioners did their work with vigor and dispatch and framed a picture of monastic corruption
sufficiently black to justify the most drastic measures. This picture was presented to parliament in
1536 with the result that all the smaller monasteries, those with an annual income of less than
£200 (some 376 all told), were dissolved and

their property, real and personal, turned over to the king. That was the first step. The second step followed the suppression of the Pilgrimage of Grace, when one after another on various charges and by various methods the larger monasteries were also done away with. All this, much of it of very dubious legality, was confirmed by act of parliament in 1539.

And now Cromwell could fulfill his promise, for the monastic confiscations brought to his master something like one-sixth of all the land of England, yielding an annual rental of at least £100,000. The business of liquidating this enormous property stretched out over the rest of the reign. We have record of something like one thousand separate grantees who paid to the king for their concessions something like £800,000. This accounted for about two-thirds of the total, the other third, or most of it, was apparently let out on lease. It ought to be remarked that many of the original grantees bought only to sell again, often in many parcels, and that in consequence the number of those who were interested parties to the transaction was much greater than one thousand and included representatives of all classes. It ought also to be remarked that Henry had spent all that he had received from the sales before the end of his reign and that the only residue left to the crown was the third which it had out on lease. This constituted a reserve which probably saved England from bankruptcy in the long wars against Spain at the end of the century.

It is not easy to overestimate the economic and social consequences of a measure which precipitated the whole monastic population upon the community and in the course of a few years transferred nearly 20 per cent of all the land of England to new owners. As for the personnel, the heads of the houses were on the whole well treated. In addition to pensions and gratuities many of the abbots were appointed to high positions in the secular church. A dozen of them became bishops, another dozen deans, not to mention lesser appointments. The provision for the rank and file was, if not ample, at least sufficient. The monks got pensions and a large number of them were in time provided with benefices. As for the nuns, they perhaps suffered most, but they got pensions also and in time many of them married.

The broader political and social consequences of the dissolution cannot be measured so accurately, but they are of fundamental importance. Immediately, the passing of the abbots removed half of the ecclesiastics from the House of Lords. This had the effect of changing its complexion from a body which had been predominantly clerical to one predominately lay in character. No doubt this change greatly facilitated the subsequent steps in the establishment of a national church under Edward VI and again under Elizabeth.

Much more important was the passing of the ecclesiastical lands into the hands of new owners. Whether the monastic heads had been good landlords or bad they had at any rate a traditional connection with the countryside and traditional responsibilities which made them something far more than rent collectors. Their tenants were not merely sources of revenue, they were also in some sort protégés, children who must be looked after and cared for even if their rents were not forthcoming. Their broad acres were not merely so much crop-producing soil, they were also the old familiar valleys and hills of home. And now there came a new type of landlord, city bred for the most part, with an attitude towards agriculture developed in the marts of trade. Land was for them a commodity to be bought and sold, or if not sold, to be exploited for all that it might be worth. They had invested good money in it and they expected a good return. If tenant A could not pay his rent and even increase his rent, he must make way for tenant B. If the land was ill-suited for growing corn it had better be converted into pasture. They were in fact business men, eager of course to acquire the social prestige attached to the position of the land-owning country gentleman, but still business men. More and more as their influence spread business standards and business ethics displaced the older standards and the older ethics in the countryside. We should not ascribe all this to the transfer of monastic lands. A great deal of other land was changing hands in sixteenth century England through the perfectly legitimate channels of the real estate market and was being bought up by the prosperous bourgeoisie. We shall note this more particularly when we come to consider the rapid growth of the enclosure movement by which a large part of arable England was being converted into sheep pasture. No movement of the time was so easy to justify on economic grounds, no move-ment perhaps so disastrous in its social conse-quences.

A great deal has been made of the part played by the monasteries in ministering to the relief of the poor. The rapid development of the problem of poverty in sixteenth century England has often been ascribed to the sudden cessation of monastic charity. This is very doubtfully true. Indeed it may well be questioned whether the indiscriminate alms-giving which characterized monastic benevolence did not do more to pauperize than to alleviate poverty.

From the point of view of the maintenance of Henry's ecclesiastical arrangements, the wide distribution of monastic property was immensely important. It gave to a large number of influential Englishmen a definite stake in the break from Rome. Later, when Queen Mary restored the old faith in England she found it impossible to recover the monastic lands. How much the fear that they might be recovered had to do with stimulating the zeal of the bourgeoisie for Protestantism can never be ascertained until we find some way of determining the relative weight of economic and religious interests in the calculations of the sixteenth century Englishman.

It was directly after Cromwell had completed his first step in the dissolution of the monasteries that Henry had to face the only serious revolt against his government in the whole course of his reign. It went by the name of the Pilgrimage of Grace, started in Lincolnshire in the autumn of 1536, spread to Yorkshire and the further north almost immediately and was over before Christmas. At one time it mustered as many as forty thousand rebels under its banners and undertook to dictate terms even to Henry himself. It was set going by the despoiling of the monasteries, by a new levy of taxes and by a fresh visitation of the clergy. But it presently drew within its rank almost every type of discontent—discontent of the nobles at the upstarts in the king's council, discontent of the gentry at legislation hostile to their interests, enacted by remote parliaments packed with royal officials, discontent of the commons with taxes, enclosures, rack-rents, rising prices and other economic ills. The fundamental issue was perhaps that between a north, not yet quite conscious of its nationalism, a north still feudal, still Roman Catholic, still loyal to pre-Tudor conceptions of church and state, and a south which had marched with the progress of the times. The religious question was the one point of common agreement but there was no real unity of purpose and certainly no intelligent program of action. The rebels were desperately anxious to prove that they were not rebels and they threw away every chance of success by their reluctance to fight even when they had at command an overwhelming preponderance of armed force. Henry handled the situation if not honestly at least cleverly and brought the rebels to disband their ranks by promises of redress and pardon which he probably never seriously intended

[81]

to keep. In the end the pilgrimage achieved none of its objectives. It rather quickened than retarded the final break from Rome; it not only did not save the smaller monasteries but it provoked the destruction of the larger ones. It left the law and parliament and the council and Thomas Cromwell undisturbed. What it did do was to reveal a dangerous situation in the north which led Henry the next year to establish a Council of the North Parts. We should not be far wrong if we regarded this as a branch office of the privy council, designed to give to the region north of the Trent a lively sense of the reality of the royal power and a comfortable sense of its efficiency and its devotion to the common welfare. In the end it served all of these purposes and drew the north by degrees into the well-ordered administrative system of the south.

"The crushing of the Pilgrimage of Grace was Henry VIII's Arbela: after that he moved whether he would and had really conquered both worlds." The death of Katherine of Aragon and of Anne Boleyn in the same year—the first by natural causes, the second by the executioner's sword for conjugal infidelity—simplified his problem still further. So long as Katherine lived she constituted a standing obstacle to any close agreement between England and the Empire. "God be praised,"

Henry had remarked when he heard of her demise, "we are free from all suspicion of war." Anne's death set him free to marry again and establish a line the legitimacy of which could not be open to question by either Catholic or Protestant. Already he had picked out Anne's successor and on the very day that she was beheaded he secured a license from Cranmer to marry Jane Seymour, a pale, modest, gentle-souled maiden, some twenty years his junior. Jane lived just long enough to bear Henry a son. That again simplified many problems, for Henry's two surviving children, Mary and Elizabeth, had both of them been declared illegitimate and so incompetent to succeed to the throne. In short, by the beginning of the year 1537 Henry had established his kingdom, established his church, established his line. The rest of the story of his reign, if not without color, is relatively without significance. He continued to function with parliament and found parliament ready to do his will. Much has been made of the Statute of Proclamations, passed in 1539, which gave to the royal proclamations the force of law, but its importance in contributing to the royal prerogative has been exaggerated. It may well be argued that by giving to proclamations a definite statutory basis it substituted for divine right parliamentary sanction.

Rather more important was the Act of Succession of 1536, somewhat modified by the later one of 1544, which placed in Henry's hands the right to determine the order of succession to the throne by will. Here was certainly a demonstration of his plenitude of power, yet here again parliament was establishing through the king its control over matters which had customarily been regarded as ordained by God. In both cases certainly the readiness of parliament to support Henry and to give him virtually everything he asked for is sufficiently apparent. The machinery of government by consent was working smoothly and continued to work smoothly as long as Henry lived, though parliament still had to be managed and parliamentary elections more or less controlled. The relative ease with which Henry got the large grants of money he wanted for his Scottish and French wars during the closing years of his reign is particularly notable. He was also allowed to collect benevolences and to manipulate the currency practically without remonstrance. Of course there was grumbling, there always is grumbling when the payment of taxes is in question. But there was no concerted, effective grumbling, no real indication that Bluff King Hal was losing his firm grip upon the loyal support of his subjects.

In the closer cabinet of Henry's ministers the outstanding episode of the last ten years of the reign was the fall of Cromwell. It was death to the man himself, it was death also to the vicarious system of government of which, under Henry, he had been the second great exponent. Cromwell never quite reached the pinnacle that Wolsey had attained. He had never been lord chancellor, he had never been papal legate, though as vicar-general he came as near to it as he well could come after the break from Rome. On the other hand he was, what Wolsey always disdained to be, a clever and competent parliamentarian. For that reason he may be accredited with a more significant contribution to English constitutional development than Wolsey ever made. Like Wolsey he was more than prime minister—he was sole minister. And as with Wolsey the height of his preëminence tended to reduce his colleagues in the privy council to mere puppets. They walked under his huge legs and peered about to find themselves dishonorable graves.

With Cromwell's fall Henry become his own prime minister and restored his council to something like its normal functioning. It did more supervisory work, it became more like a board of directors. It began, for instance, to keep minutes.

There were some nineteen members, most of them high officials. Stephen Gardiner, bishop of Winchester, was, after Cromwell's fall, probably the outstanding man, unless it was Thomas Howard, duke of Norfolk. Edward Seymour, earl of Hertford, Henry's brother-in-law, and Thomas Cranmer, the archbishop, commanded probably the largest measure of the royal confidence. Henry always had a singularly tender spot in his heart for Cranmer, a curious fact when we consider how widely the two men differed in temper. The whole group was very far from being homogeneous. Henry took no pains to make it so; like his daughter Elizabeth after him, he preferred to be surrounded by men of differing opinions. There was in consequence a good deal of personal rivalry and backbiting with a broad line of cleavage between a faction led by Norfolk and Gardiner who thought the reformation in religion had gone far enough, and a faction led by Hertford and Cranmer who wanted to lead it some distance farther.

The immediate reason for Cromwell's fall was his fear of a combination of Habsburg and Valois against England and his consequent endeavor to strengthen Henry's position by an alliance with the German Protestant princes. This took concrete form in the arrangement of a marriage for the king with Anne of Cleves but it involved also a rather definite *rapprochement* to a more distinctly Protestant position. Here if anywhere we get indications of Cromwell's sympathetic attitude towards the reformers. The break from Rome had not yet disclosed any marked break with the Roman theology. Some attempt had been made to define the official creed in Ten Articles which had been drafted by the king and accepted by convocation in 1536, but they were vague upon many points and they lacked parliamentary confirmation. They revealed some Protestant influence and coming as they did in the year that marked the beginning of the attack on the monasteries, and coming from the king, they gave hope to the reformers of better things. Two years later Cromwell issued a series of injunctions which mark a further advance in the same direction. The English Bible was to be set up in all the churches, the Lord's Prayer, the Creed and the Commandments were to be taught in English, sermons were to be preached, images to be taken down. To add fuel to the flames, the hoax of the rood of Boxley was exposed with all its wretched mechanism of wood and wire, and the shrines of Our Lady of Walsingham and of Saint Thomas of Canterbury were plundered and destroyed.

All this Henry had allowed and even approved but he prided himself on his orthodoxy and he had an uneasy feeling that he was being pushed ahead faster than he wished to go. As for Anne of Cleves, after he had seen her and tried manfully to follow her broken English, he liked her not. However, seeing no escape, he went through with the marriage, only to discover that Cromwell's foreign fears were not solidly grounded and that Anne— the "Flanders mare," he called her—was quite unbearable. After that it did not take Henry long to discover that he had had enough of Cromwell. The man had no friends and once the royal support was withdrawn his fall was sure. It was the irony of fate that parliament, whose place in the state he had done so much to establish, should have dealt the final blow. He was condemned, unheard, by a bill of attainder and his head was cut off.

Anne herself proved to be quite amenable to reason. She consented to an annulment of her marriage on grounds which need not detain us, accepted a comfortable pension and remained in England, busy with her needlework, at which she was very proficient, until her death in 1557.

Cromwell's fall was a definite triumph for Gardiner and Norfolk and the conservatives, who hastened to solidify their position by providing

Henry with a new wife, Katherine Howard, a niece of Norfolk's, the second of his nieces to be royal consort. They had already succeeded in getting through parliament a declaration of faith which was a model of rigid orthodoxy. Transubstantiation, auricular confession, celibacy of the clergy, communion in one kind—all the essential points of the Roman Catholic credo were imposed upon England by law and under pain of heavy penalties. These Six Articles were England's first statutory definition of creed, her first Act of Uniformity. They did not pass without fierce debate and Henry himself came down to the upper house to support them. But they passed and recorded the king's definite veto upon any further toying with heretical notions.

That position, confirmed, strengthened and extended four years later by the so-called King's Book, remained the official position so long as Henry lived. But one must always distinguish under the Tudors between the law as it was recorded and the law as it was applied. This much is pretty clear that, notwithstanding the Six Articles and the King's Book, the conservatives on the whole lost ground during the last years of Henry's life. Perhaps the fall of Katherine Howard had something to do with it. She was the second of

Henry's wives to die at the hands of the executioner for conjugal infidelity. Probably his final marriage with Catherine Parr had even more to do with it. She was a gentle, cultured woman, beyond reproach in that fierce, licentious court, very careful of her irascible old husband and very tactful in dealing with him. She had pretty definitely Protestant sympathies—so much so that Gardiner and the conservatives actively conspired to be rid of her. In her careful, tentative way she probably did something to modify the king's attitude. Cranmer's influence was in the same direction and Hertford's as well. As for the conservatives, notwithstanding Henry's sympathy with their religious position, they somehow never really established themselves in his confidence. Henry maintained them against their rivals but when he came to make plans for the government of his son he left them out. Gardiner's name was deliberately omitted from the list of executors of his will and the Howards, father and son, Norfolk and Surrey, the soldier and the poet, were being hustled to the block, convicted traitors, when Henry was on his deathbed. Surrey suffered the extreme penalty; Norfolk escaped, but just escaped, because death reached Henry first. Those to whom he left his son in charge were most of them reformers.

In Henry's foreign policy we mark three distinct periods. Under Wolsey the objective appears to have been to promote England's prestige in European affairs; under Cromwell, to keep England safe from foreign interference while Henry set his church in order; after Cromwell's fall, to establish England's hegemony in the British Isles. Henry's purposes became more and more distinctly British as he grew older and his relations with his continental neighbors became more and more definitely shaped with reference to British problems. He might be treating with Habsburg and fighting against Valois as indeed he was, but it was of Wales he was thinking and Ireland and Scotland, or rather it was of a British empire compacted of all of them.

The Welsh problem was comparatively simple. It involved no foreign entanglements and offered no national resistance. As a matter of fact no part of Britain was more passionately loyal to the Tudors than Wales was. After all, were not the Tudors Welshmen? But Wales and the English counties bordering on Wales were hotbeds of disorder and a standing menace to the safety of life and property on England's western front. The trouble was that Wales had no orderly system of government but still remained under a régime

partly feudal and partly tribal, transmitted from
the dark ages with the primitive standards of the
dark ages. Henry took the problem in hand in
1536 and by act of parliament definitely incorporated Wales with England. He converted the
lawless regalities into shires and subjected them to
the English law with all the paraphernalia of
English justice. And over all he set a Council of
the Marches of Wales, another branch office of the
privy council with commensurate powers. This
was the first act of union in English history and,
though it was pretty frankly intended as a police
measure, the first step towards the realization of
an imperial design.

The Irish problem was not so simple. There
were seas to cross and no family loyalties to invoke.
The Irish were not definitely anti-English, they
were not definitely a unit for any purpose. Two-
thirds of them were still wild clansmen who ac-
knowledged no government except that of their
clan and recognized no law except tribal custom.
England had been trying in some sort to govern
them for centuries and had succeeded in carving
out a segment along the eastern coast known as
the Pale where the inhabitants paid at least lip
service to the king. Within the Pale there was even
a parliament and a lord deputy and laws in abun-

dance. But none of it amounted to much and the only thing which saved the English rule from extinction was that the Irish were too busy quarreling among themselves to form a united front against any common enemy.

Henry, during the early years of his reign, was disposed to allow the Irish to stew in their own juice. There seemed nothing else to do unless he was prepared to spend a great deal of time, energy and money in reducing them to order and good government, and the matter did not interest him that much. But after the break from Rome the Irish question took on a different complexion. Irish rebels began to look to the emperor for assistance and Charles V found it desirable to cultivate their good will. Ireland in fact revealed itself as a possible base for hostile operations against England and its more effective control became necessary if only as a measure of national defense. Henry in consequence proceeded to deal with Ireland vigorously. He defined a policy which contemplated the establishment in Ireland of English justice, the English language and the English system of land tenure. He met the papal claims of suzerainty by having the Irish parliament change his title from Lord to King of Ireland and he induced many of the more powerful chiefs to relinquish their tribal independence in return for English titles. All this marked the beginning of a new epoch in Irish history, brought a long period of inaction to a close and inaugurated a policy of active intervention which was to lead eventually to the complete subjugation of the island. For the time being at least Henry was extraordinarily successful and when he died Ireland seemed to be on the point of entering an era of peace and prosperity. He was mercifully spared a vision of the long and hideous sequel.

Both the Welsh and the Irish problems theoretically at least fall within the category of internal affairs. Scotland was quite a different matter. Since Edward I's time English kings had laid claim to the suzerainty of Scotland and had at intervals secured some sort of confirmation of their claim from Scottish kings. But the Scots had successfully resisted various attempts to absorb them into the English state. In fact if there was any one clear, dominant note in the confused politics of the northern kingdom it was the maintenance of its independence as against England. This led eventually to a close relation between Scotland and England's perennial continental enemy, France. Henry VII made, as we have seen, a very definite effort to cultivate Scottish good will and gave the hand of his elder daughter, Margaret, in marriage to the Scottish king. It was this marriage in the end that solved the problem, but the fruits of it were long a-ripening. "Immediately it did nothing to avert and little to soothe the friction between the two countries." When Henry VIII came to the throne Scotland was far from friendly and when he went to France on his first campaign in 1513 the Scots attempted an invasion of England on a scale quite unprecedented. They were disastrously defeated at Flodden and their king himself fell on the field of battle. But nothing came of it except to exacerbate feeling. Henry made no effort to follow up this advantage and during the ensuing twenty years contented himself simply with preventing a formidable combination of Scotland with France. The notion of solving the problem by annexation and absorption did not apparently enter his mind.

After Cromwell's fall there are definite indications of a change in attitude. This was no doubt partly due to the break from Rome, which added to all the other issues between England and Scotland the issue of religion. It was partly due also to the increasing menace of a combination of all the Catholic powers against England, the fear of which, as we have seen, brought about the Cleves

fiasco and Cromwell's undoing. Henry was im-
pressed with the importance of consolidating his
position. If his foreign policy after 1540 was aggressive in appearance it was defensive in purpose.
His expensive wars with France in the closing
years of his reign really reflect a reversal of the
time-worn maxim. It was no longer: "Who France
will win must with Scotland first begin." It was
rather: "Who Scotland will win must with
France," etc. Scotland, not France, was in fact the
real objective and the severance of the Franco-
Scottish alliance his immediate purpose.

He had for some time been pressing James V,
the young chivalrous Scottish king, to follow his
own example—cast off the Roman yoke and seize
the property of the church. In 1536 he tried to
induce James to meet him at York and talk things
over. But James was fearful and instead of falling
in with Henry's plans took ship for France and
married the daughter of the French king. His
wife died within a year, but he presently found
another French one, this time Mary of Lorraine,
daughter of the duke of Guise. The net result of
Henry's friendly gesture was in short to drive
Scotland farther from England and nearer to
France than ever. And his subsequent efforts to
countercheck French influence in the north by

peaceful persuasion accomplished nothing. Meanwhile, as always, the endemic border warfare offered plenty of excuses for armed conflict. In August 1542 a band of English raiders in Teviotdale was set upon and badly defeated. Henry seized upon this as a *casus belli*. He insisted that Scotland should make reparation, sign a perpetual league and send her king to London to ratify it. James declined and an English army marched across the border in October. It did no more than burn a few insignificant villages. The counterstroke by the Scots was much more disastrous. Some eighteen thousand of them were cut to pieces at Solway Moss by an English force of less than a quarter their number. It was a humiliating defeat, more humiliating, because of the inequality of the forces engaged, than Flodden Field. The news of it killed the Scottish king and exposed his kingdom, practically defenseless, to Henry's mercy.

Had he been wise he would have been moderate and have laid a firm foundation for the union of the two kingdoms by arranging a marriage between Edward, his infant son, and the infant daughter of the dead James, Mary Queen of Scots. The match was indeed provided for by treaty but Henry insisted upon more than that. He insisted upon a recognition by the Scots of the old English claim of suzerainty. And so he drove Scotland once more into the arms of France. The result was a war upon both fronts, the most expensive of all the wars Henry fought and the most futile. His armies harried the border and destroyed Edinburgh, captured Boulogne and held it against every effort of the French to dislodge them. His navy beat off a rather formidable attack by a large French armada on the south coast. But it all amounted to little or nothing though it consumed two-thirds of all the plunder of the monasteries and very large amounts raised by taxation besides. Scotland was no more English when it was over than when it began. It was to become even more French before it became less so. Yet during this troubled period forces were germinating in Scotland which were to prove more potent in destroying the Franco-Scottish alliance than all the operations of hostile English armies put together. Just before the war was over George Wishart, first of the Scottish Protestant martyrs, was burned at the stake and Cardinal Beaton, last of the great Scottish Catholic prelates, was assassinated and the issue between the old church and the new was definitely joined. John Knox would follow presently with his "hot gospelers" and within fifteen years France and Rome together would be set packing out of Scotland. This was not the way Henry intended it and it can hardly be maintained that he was in any direct way responsible for it, though he did have his share in Beaton's assassination and he had realized that a breach between Scotland and Rome would almost inevitably open a breach between Scotland and France.

Peace came in June 1546. Less than a year later Henry died, being then in his fifty-fifth year. He had ruled over England for nearly forty years during one of the most momentous periods in her history. And though he had many great men about him he had dominated his government up to almost the very moment of his passing. What was done was in the ultimate analysis his work; the most important factor in every public decision was his opinion, his will. No one ever questioned that, not even Wolsey for all his pride of place. Henry was indeed a great ruler of men. He was also a great popular leader. He understood to a remarkable degree the art of popular appeal, and that was fundamentally because he understood the English and devoted himself to their service. It is easy to multiply instances of his cruelty to individuals but no king was ever more careful of the interests of the rank and file of his subjects. His greatest contribution to English constitutional development was the definite establishment of parliament as an essential part of the machinery of government.

England throve and prospered under him and notwithstanding all the burden of his wars was a vastly richer country at his death than it had been at his accession. That was perhaps the best of all reasons for his popularity. In any event he did succeed in creating in the English mind an attitude of loyalty to his dynasty strong enough to carry through all the distractions of Edward's and Mary's reigns and to find its supreme expression in the universal devotion to his second daughter, Elizabeth.

EDWARD VI

CHAPTER III

EDWARD VI

HEN Henry VIII died, Edward, his one legitimate son, was only ten years old. Henry had realized before his death that he would not live until Edward was old enough to reign in his own right and the thought had troubled him not a little. Woe indeed to that land whose king is a child, particularly a land with only two generations between it and the disordered times of the Wars of the Roses. The old king devoted almost his last conscious hours to the business of providing an adequate government for a royal minority. He selected sixteen of his wisest ministers and formed them into a council of regency, being careful to include conservatives and progressives, Catholics and Protestants, and to omit the extremists of both camps. But there was no exact balance of power; the strong men of the regency were, if not ardent reformers, certainly not averse to change. The outstanding figure among them was Edward Seymour, earl of Hertford, soon to become duke of Somerset, the young king's uncle, and next to him John Dudley, earl of Warwick, later to be duke of Northumberland. There was Cranmer also, of course, and to counterbalance his Zwinglian propensities, Wriothesley, the lord chancellor, a hater of heretics. Of the rest none stands out preëminently. It should be noted that the three tutors selected by Henry for his son were all of them prominent Protestant reformers.

These arrangements did not stand for long. At the very first meeting of the new council Seymour was named lord protector and by degrees he managed to concentrate the royal power in his own hands and to reduce his colleagues to a subordinate position. In fact the first three years of Edward's reign was really the reign of his uncle just as the last three years was really the reign of John Dudley, though Dudley never formally assumed the title of lord protector.

As for the young king, he acquiesced in all these changing arrangements without protest but also without enthusiasm. He was healthy enough, but was never robust like his father. He was in fact a bookish, rather religious, rather solitary person. We have letters of his and a journal full of coldblooded comments about the battles, murders and sudden deaths taking place all about him. We have also, in the last year of his life, a discourse on the reformation of abuses which reveals an alertness to the current vices of the age and a disposition to correct them. But time did not serve and Edward in fact left no mark at all upon public policy. He does not seem to have aroused any enthusiasm among his subjects. Holbein painted him more than once and so he lives for us in the flesh, but as a factor in the history of his times he is negligible. After all he was only ten when he began to reign and only sixteen when he died—a mere boy, and towards the end a very sickly boy with a hard racking cough.

He had been committed at the age of six to a marriage with Mary Stuart. Henry VIII, as we have seen, devoted a good deal of energy during the closing years of his life to the business of establishing friendly relations with Scotland and breaking up the old Franco-Scottish alliance. He had accomplished less than nothing. When he died a French regent, Mary of Guise, was governing Scotland, French troops were besieging Saint Andrews, the last stronghold of the English faction there, and a French expedition was making ready to descend upon the coast and carry off the young Scottish queen. Henry on his death-bed had planned another invasion of Scotland and is said to have urged the task with his dying breath upon Seymour. Be this as it may, Seymour took up the Scottish problem as soon as he came to power. He would have liked to unite the two countries peacefully by consent and by marriage as already arranged. But the French were on the ground and the Scots, supported by their presence, were in a brave fighting mood. They made no answer to Seymour's offers to treat. He saw no other way to his objectives than by armed invasion. In September 1547 he crossed the border, to fight at Pinkie Cleuch "the last and the bloodiest of the battles between the two independent kingdoms." Once more the Scots suffered a decisive defeat and once more English garrisons covered the country almost to the walls of Edinburgh. And once more nothing at all came of it in the way of drawing the two countries closer together. The very next year the French carried off the young Scottish queen, the affianced bride of the French dauphin, to be reared in France against her wedding day. The best thing the English did for their cause was to ship cartloads of English Bibles over the border.

There was work aplenty awaiting Seymour when he got back to England. In October 1547 he opened his first parliament. It seems to have been freely elected—there is at any rate no evidence to indicate the contrary—and that fact is important because it supports the conclusion that the legislation which ensued was, if not popularly conceived, at least popularly supported. It had to do mainly, as might be expected, with matters ecclesiastical. It swept away the old laws against heresy, and Henry VIII's Six Articles and all legal restrictions upon reading, teaching and expounding the Scriptures. In short, it opened the door to change without itself dictating change. Parliamentary action in these matters did little more than confirm what had already been done by act of council. A book of homilies had been put forth and injunctions had been issued which called upon the preachers to preach against Rome and enjoined the faithful to do away with the superstitious images and pictures on the walls and in the windows of the churches. And the preachers had responded with zeal and the iconoclasts had begun the work which, before it was finished, was to reduce the lovely, colorful parish churches of England to the level of naked, whitewashed Quaker meeting houses.

Presently the church service itself was handed over to a commission, with Cranmer at its head, for revision. A draft Book of Common Prayer was the result, prepared chiefly by Cranmer himself. It was submitted to parliament for approval and after much debate and some amendment was adopted as the official definition of the established church and imposed upon the English clergy by the First Act of Uniformity. It was never ratified by the clergy themselves in convocation. We must regard it therefore as definitely imposed by the State—a complete triumph of the Erastian theory of church government. The fact that parliament itself approved may be taken to register national assent. The penalties imposed upon nonconformity were mild, singularly mild, considering the age and generation. No other churches were recognized and the clergy were forbidden to use any other service under penalty of fine and imprisonment. As for the laity, they might think as they pleased so long as they did not disturb the establishment or hold public worship in any other form. "It was the mildest Act of Uniformity which ever bore that unhappy name."

The prayerbook itself measured a relatively short dissenting step from the Henrican Catholicism which had prevailed in England for over ten years. It was based upon the old Catholic servicebooks and was instinct with the spirit of the Catholic church. It revealed no traces of contemporary heresy. Something was added from Lutheran sources but not in any spirit of revolt against those elements which "had behind them fifteen hundred years of Christian thought." The changes made were in the direction of bringing out more clearly the significance of a liturgy to worshipers for the most part illiterate, in the direction of admitting the congregation to a larger share in the ritual. The great change was in the translation from the Latin to the English tongue. A book which had been confined to the learned was now open to every English person who could hear or read. And it was set forth in prose which displays as well perhaps as any words ever written the richness and beauty of the English language. It was destined to become something more than a contemporary statement of a contemporary position in the Anglican church. It was destined to be recognized as the finest vehicle of devotion in English and to carry spiritual consolation far beyond the frontiers which circumscribed the Anglican communion.

Notwithstanding all its merits, the new prayer-book did not satisfy everyone. The more radical reformers, released by the repeal of the old laws from the fear of heresy, set about at once agitating for further changes in the direction away from Rome. The Catholics, who managed to swallow the royal supremacy so long as they could have the old ritual, would have none of the new service. The peasantry in the southwest of England rose in revolt under their priests, gathered together in a formidable array and laid siege to the city of Exeter. They demanded the restoration of the Six Articles, of the Latin mass, of the sacrament administered as it had been. They protested against the service in English, which was after all to the average Cornishman an outlandish and unintelligible tongue. It was only through the use of foreign mercenaries that the siege was raised and the uprising suppressed. Another uprising of the same sort broke forth in Oxfordshire. It was ultimately put down with ruthless severity and the hanging of scores of priests from their own church spires. It alarmed the government to the point of destroying bridges to check a march on London.

Yet it was clear enough that the great majority of Englishmen were quite willing to accept the new ecclesiastical arrangements. Much more alarming was the widespread social unrest. All over England men were complaining of hard times and rising prices, of greedy bankers and landlords and speculators. Preachers were thundering against the vices of the times in the pulpits and writers were recording dreams of a "very and true commonwealth," knit together by a common devotion to a common good and quite free of the greed and commercialism which seemed to be the dominating motives in the world about them. It is surprising to find, in an age apparently so much preoccupied with matters of religion, so much talking and thinking about matters fundamentally social and economic. The fact is that Englishmen found themselves in a rapidly changing world and experienced no little difficulty in adjusting themselves to it. With the expansion of foreign trade, medieval industrial and commercial arrangements, designed for an urban or at most a national economy, were breaking down. The democratic ideals of the craft-guilds were giving way to sharp distinctions between employer and employee, capital and labor. In the countryside the medieval manor with its antiquated provision for a rotation of customary crops and its commons and waste was being converted into sheep pasture to cater to the lucrative market for English wool. Old forms remained, old laws remained, but the forms and the laws were no longer consonant with the operating, productive forces of the land and so no longer applicable and in large measure no longer applied. That was perhaps fundamentally the trouble. Men still looked to the old laws for protection against the iniquities of the new arrangements and looked

in vain. And the best that the social reformers
could offer were either impossible utopias or a
return to the good old days.

Among all the evils of the times those two
which provoked the bitterest protest were the rise
in prices and the Enclosure movement. In part the
rise in prices was inevitable and proceeded from
causes quite beyond English control, notably the
increase in the supply of precious metals consequent upon the opening up of the mines of Mexico
and Peru. But this factor operated indiscriminately
all over the European market. What irritated
Englishmen just at this time was that English
prices were out of line with prices prevalent elsewhere. The cause for this was not far to seek. It
was directly due to the inflation of the currency
which began under Henry VIII and was carried
considerably further under Edward VI. It took the
form of an increase in the amount of alloy in English coins and went to such lengths that in the end
not more than a quarter of the English shilling was
precious metal. The effect, of course, was to drive
the good money overseas or out of circulation and
to weaken the credit of the government in the Antwerp money market to a point where it had to pay
15 to 20 per cent interest on its outstanding loans.
But what the average Englishman felt was the

rise in prices, particularly since it affected commodities much more than it did wages.

More serious was the issue over enclosures. The old manorial arrangement designed for the cultivation of the soil was an open field system, in which the holdings of the individual tenants were in scattered strips. Appendant to each holding in the arable land were certain rights of pasturage on common land. In operation the manor was a community enterprise in which the court of the manor regulated the crop and the seedtime and harvest. There was no chance at all for individual enterprise and only so much chance for grazing as the common lands afforded. The manor supported a considerable population which was virtually self-sustaining but which produced little or no surplus for an outside market. Tenants held their lands on various terms from the lord of the manor; in the great majority of cases rents were fixed by custom and became less and less valuable as commodity prices went up. The lord of the manor had every economic inducement to change these arrangements particularly since he was well assured that if he could convert arable into pasture land he could get a much handsomer return from his estates. In consequence there was a steady effort by the landlords to get rid of their customary tenants one way

or another and to go into the sheep-raising business. This was notably true of the new town-bred
gentry who had taken over the monastic lands.
The government did what it could to oppose this
tendency for a number of reasons, the principal
one being that it was operating to destroy the
sturdy yeomanry, still regarded as the backbone of
the English army. It was also breeding rebellion.
In the summer of 1549, for example, there were
sporadic uprisings in most of the southern counties,
and one even as far north as Yorkshire. The most
serious one was in Norfolk. It began with an un-
organized tearing down of hedges by a crowd of
indignant rustics at the end of a holiday but took
on much more serious proportions when Robert
Kett, one of the local gentry, put himself at the
head of it and gathered a force of something like
16,000 men on a hill just outside the city of Nor-
wich. For some weeks Kett and his followers "dictated communistic law" to a large part of East
Anglia, feeding themselves by systematic plunder
of the neighboring landlords.

The government was alarmed. Somerset himself
would have been content with a very shadowy submission followed by a general pardon. He was
strongly hostile to the enclosing landlords. But
open rebellion could not be tolerated. In conse-

quence he sent an army under Dudley into Norfolk in August, an army made up mostly of foreign mercenaries. It was successful as it was almost certain to be against the untrained and ill-equipped peasantry. In a pitched battle some 3,000 of Kett's men were killed and he himself was taken and executed.

And so the most considerable uprising in Edward's reign came to nothing. It served to reveal a very definite rift in the royal council between Somerset, who wished to enforce vigorously the laws against enclosure, and the landlord party under Dudley's leadership. Somerset had plenty of enemies. He was blamed in general for the disordered state of England. He was condemned by the Catholics for being too Protestant and by the Protestants for not being Protestant enough. The well-to-do hated his social policy; if he had friends among the poor they were powerless to help him. In October he was forced to resign his office.

It was not clear at first what kind of government would succeed him. The Catholics cherished a definite hope of a religious reaction, but it presently became apparent that religion had little to do with the issue. The one tie which united the diverse elements against Somerset was opposition to his social and economic policy. Legislation passed in the parliament which met in November 1549 made this clear enough. It was aimed to check rebellion, to prevent unlawful assemblies and, most notable of all, to permit enclosures. Nothing at all was done for the Catholics. Before the autumn was out their most important adherents in the council were placed under restraint. In fact Dudley, whatever his private sympathies may have been (on the scaffold later he professed to be a Catholic), presently revealed his intention to go a good deal further in the opposite direction.

As a preliminary, and because the exchequer was empty, he came to terms with France, yielding up Boulogne to her for money and conceding to her a free hand with Scotland. Boulogne did not matter. England was better off without it, though she might have got a better price for it than she did. But to hand over Scotland to the French was to abandon one of the fundamental principles of Tudor policy. However, there appeared to be no immediate help for it. At any rate it delivered England from a war on two fronts and an intolerable drain upon her resources.

All that Dudley's government did immediately about the religious problem was to enforce the Act of Uniformity against the clergy. There was no real persecution. The Roman martyrologists could not number as many as ten who suffered for their faith in the whole of Edward's reign, and of those not one had to endure more than deprivation and imprisonment. Six bishops were removed and their places filled with ardent reformers. Ridley, who became Bishop of London, and Hooper, "father of nonconformity," the new Bishop of Gloucester, were the outstanding ones. It was Hooper who began the attack upon episcopal vestments which was to develop later into the Vestiarian controversy. It was Ridley who insisted that the Catholic altars at the east end of the church should be replaced by communion tables in the body of the church. And it was from Ridley's pulpit in St. Paul's that the doctrine of transubstantiation, which asserted the Real Presence of the body and blood of Christ in the sacrament of the Lord's Supper, was officially condemned. Meanwhile Thomas Cranmer, assisted by foreign divines, was busy revising the prayer-book in the same spirit. It was to be adopted by parliament two years later. This so-called second prayer-book represents the extreme point to which the Church of England ever went in the direction of Zwinglianism and Calvinism. Admittedly it was a compromise. Many of the features in the first prayer-book which had tended to identify it with the Latin mass were deliberately changed as a concession to the radicals. To them, also, was yielded the doctrine of the Real Presence. And yet the main features of the earlier ritual and the earlier teaching were left to reassure the conservatives. And the old church government was left intact.

It can hardly be doubted that the spirit which dictated this revision was rather political than spiritual. Dudley, who desperately feared a reaction when Edward should die and his Catholic sister Mary should succeed, wished to consolidate into one band the Protestants of all complexions, and particularly to gather into the fold of the establishment the "hot gospelers" like Hooper and Ridley and John Knox, who were the fighting strength of the Protestant cause.

"The second prayer-book never had the slightest chance to any ecclesiastical authority; it was only in force about eight months and probably was never used at all in many parts of England." It is to be noted, however, that parliament imposed it under rather heavy penalties upon both clergy and laity. The so-called Second Act of Uniformity was much more drastic than the first. It not only forbade any other form of service but it undertook to compel men to accept the established one. Recusancy, that is to say, refusal to attend the state church, became definitely punishable and the recusant, who was later to become a very familiar figure in English history, makes at this time his début upon the scene.

These religious changes had their seamy side. The mercenary motive was never far from Dudley and his greedy colleagues. Most of the new bishops had to surrender part of their episcopal lands to the courtiers as a price for their elevation. The simplification of the ritual, by dispensing with the need for ecclesiastical ornaments, gave excuse for wholesale confiscation of the silver plate of the churches, much of which fell into private hands. The condemned lands of the chantries followed a like course. It had been intended that a large part of the revenues derived from this source should be applied to the setting up of schools and the further endowment of the universities, but most of it got diverted elsewhere. "The fortunes of many private families were raised on funds intended for national education." A good deal has been made of Edward VI's schools. As a matter of fact his government did little more than provide annual pensions for schools already established whose endowments had been confiscated.

Meanwhile Somerset had been disposed of. After his enforced resignation from the protector-

ship in 1549 he had been imprisoned for a time
in the Tower, but he had later been released and
had resumed his place, albeit no longer the chief
place, at the council table. His position there soon
proved to be an impossible one. Since he would not
submit to be Dudley's tool he inevitably became
the focal point of opposition to Dudley's policy.
The outcome was that for two years the privy
council was distracted between the two of them.
Dudley dominated the situation when he was present; when he was absent Somerset was the commanding figure. And Somerset was stronger in the
country and in parliament. Dudley had the advantage that he was more unscrupulous and that
he completely controlled the young king. In October 1551 the blow fell. Somerset in the previous
spring had made a half-hearted attempt to change
the government and had intended to summon parliament for the purpose. But that was not the
charge made against him at his trial. It really does
not matter what the charge was. Dudley admitted
later that the whole case was fabricated. In any
event Somerset was condemned to death. His execution followed in January 1552. He was a better
man every way than his rival but a curious bundle
of contradictory qualities. We have to set against
the able military commander in the field the vi-·

sionary at the council table. We have to reconcile his proud and haughty bearing towards his colleagues with his sympathetic attitude towards the peasantry. On one side he was an ambitious and rapacious courtier; on another a lover of liberty and a stout champion of social justice. He was loyal to his friends, sincere in his religious professions and he scorned to stoop to the political methods of his enemies. He fought for the common people when there were few who had the courage to fight for them. He tried in vain to stem the tide of heartless commercialism which was invading the countryside. But he lacked the energy essential to a crusader contending against desperate odds and he lacked the cleverness to cope with the unscrupulous politicians pitted against him. His great claim to distinction is that in a wicked and corrupt generation the English remembered him as "the good duke."

It was after Somerset's death that the second prayer-book came and the Second Act of Uniformity. Otherwise the last two years of Edward's short reign are without distinction—a period given over to the plunder of the churches and to the unchecked rapacity of the landlords. The behavior of Dudley and his associates went far to justify Sir Thomas More's definition of government "as a certain conspiracy of rich men procuring their own commodities under the name and title of a commonwealth."

When all the private pockets had been filled there was not enough left to meet the expenses of the state. In 1553 Dudley was forced to call a parliament. He did not have the courage to face a really representative assembly. He was too unpopular. So he sent letters around to the constituencies directing them to elect his own nominees and he created eleven new Cornish boroughs which he could depend upon to be properly subservient. Even so he did not get an assembly together to his liking. It granted him a subsidy but it displayed a disposition to attack fiscal abuses which did not set at all with his plans. He dismissed it after it had been in session for barely a month.

Meanwhile the young king was pretty evidently adying. Dudley knew well enough that he could only escape the wrath to come if he could somehow perpetuate his power beyond the king's demise. The accession of Edward's Catholic sister Mary would inevitably be fatal to him. He therefore spent the closing months of Edward's life in a desperate effort to change the course of the succession in his favor. After Mary, Henry VIII's second daughter, Elizabeth, was next in line. But she was too shrewd for Dudley's purposes. Next after her Mary Queen of Scots traced the best claim through her grandmother, Margaret, the older of Henry VII's daughters. She was affianced to the French dauphin and plainly would not do. Then came the descendants of Henry VII's younger daughter, Mary. Her daughter, who was still living, was the wife of Henry Grey, duke of Suffolk, and had three daughters, of whom the oldest was Lady Jane Grey. Dudley proceeded to marry Lady Jane to his fourth son, Guildford Dudley, and then persuaded the dying king to divert the succession to Jane by will. It was hopelessly illegal and proved to be hopelessly unpopular. Nevertheless it was so recorded in Edward's will and the judges and the councilors were coerced into confirming it by letters patent. This done, Dudley strengthened his military arrangements and waited for the end. What he failed to do was to get hold of the person of Catholic Mary. Two days before Edward died the privy council summoned her to appear at his bedside. But she was forewarned, fled away and took refuge in one of the duke of Norfolk's castles in Suffolk.

On July 6, 1553, Edward died and four days later Lady Jane Grey was proclaimed queen. There was no enthusiasm for her even in London and the privy council learned with alarm that "innumerable companies of the common people" were flocking to support Mary in Suffolk. On the eleventh they received her command to proclaim her title. Plainly she had no intention of submitting without a struggle. Dudley set out with an army to fetch her to London, but he never reached her. Hardly had he left the city before the council, in terror of their lives, deserted one after another. The city fathers followed suit and before Dudley had even reached Suffolk Mary had been proclaimed queen in London by Lady Jane's own father. Two days later Dudley disbanded his forces and yielded himself a prisoner. It was all over and the rats scattered as fast as they might to get clear of the sinking ship. When Mary entered her capital early in August England was solid behind her. As for Lady Jane, a lovely young woman, zealous for her faith, already distinguished for her learning and quite out of place in the intrigues of her unscrupulous father-in-law, she would gladly have taken leave of royalty and gone back to her books and her devotions. But she could not choose. The Tower, which for a brief nine days had been her royal palace, presently became her prison. She was not to leave it finally until she took her last sad journey to the scaffold.

MARY

MARY THE CATHOLIC

AT HER accession Mary was thirty-seven years old. She was not beautiful and she was not charming. She had a short nose, a square chin, rather hostile eyes and a rough, deep voice like a man's. Tenniel might have had her portrait before him when he drew the Queen of Hearts for *Alice in Wonderland*. Her life had been a checkered one. Until she was fifteen or thereabouts, she had been the cherished daughter of her father and the heiress presumptive to the English throne. At different times during that interval she had been pledged in marriage to the French dauphin and to the Habsburg emperor. After that had come the Divorce Case, the annulment of her mother's marriage and the stigma of bastardy. She recovered some measure of her father's favor later by signing an abject submission to his marital and ecclesiastical arrangements, but the days of her adolescence were singularly unhappy ones. She never really accepted the new

[123]

order of things. It involved a denial of her own birthright. But there was more to the matter than that. The strength of the Henrican establishment lay in its appeal to the strong national spirit of the English. That fact Mary never grasped, for one reason because she was more Spanish than English, for another because she was not nationally-minded. Her fundamental loyalties were religious and by religion she meant the church universal and the pope. She never shared the fervor of English patriotism, she was quite unconscious of the economic and social considerations which were crowding religion into a subordinate place in the reckonings of her people. In fact she lacked altogether that instinctive sensitiveness to public opinion and that alert responsiveness to it which was one of the chief assets of the Tudors.

Mary knew very well what she wanted and she fought hard to get it. What she never knew was the strength of the forces opposed to her. Perhaps she never cared to know. Certainly the welfare of England and the English was never her first consideration. Under Edward she had managed to preserve the celebration of the mass in her household despite the efforts of both Somerset and Dudley to force her acceptance of the new liturgy. And she had maintained close contacts with her cousin the emperor, so close that she tended to become the focal point for Catholic intrigue against the government. Easily the most honest of the Tudors she left men even then in no doubt about her attitude. It was clear enough at her accession that she would reëstablish Roman Catholicism if she could and would in her foreign policy favor strongly a close alliance with the Habsburgs.

Her first business was to reconstruct her council and to draw about her men whom she could trust. It is rather surprising to discover that she retained no less than twelve of Dudley's councilors. Indeed she kept too many and she added too many. The new privy council was an unwieldy body of nearly fifty. The outstanding figures were Stephen Gardiner, once again bishop of Winchester and now lord chancellor, the duke of Norfolk, who had barely escaped execution at the end of Henry's reign, and Sir William Paget. Gardiner, if anyone, was prime minister.

In her dealings with the Protestants later Mary won for herself the title *Bloody*, which does her a grave injustice. She was in fact, except when religion was in question, the most merciful of all the Tudors. This is apparent in her treatment of those who had conspired with Dudley to deprive her of her throne. Out of sixty who were denounced as traitors, only seven were brought to trial and of this seven only three, Dudley and his two principal coadjutors, Palmer and Gates, were executed. Dudley of course could not be spared, though he tried to save his neck at the end by an edifying profession of the Roman Catholic faith. He had been a desperate, unscrupulous gambler, playing for the highest stakes in the kingdom, and he had lost. A bad man, he was a bad loser. If there was anything for which he had seemed to stand it was for the Protestant faith. With his last breath he had betrayed it.

The religious question was, of course, foremost in Mary's mind. She would have liked to have re-established the Roman church in England at once and she deceived herself into believing that the reaction which had borne her so easily to the throne reflected a universal demand for a return to the Roman communion. But the imperial ambassador Renard, who probably had more influence over her at this juncture than any man in England, counseled caution. He saw plenty of evidences in London and elsewhere of deep-rooted Protestant sympathies and he realized that the great majority of Englishmen who professed and called themselves Catholics had in mind not the papacy and Rome but the old creed and the old ritual under royal supremacy—Henrican Catholicism in short. If there was anything clearer than the loyalty of the English to Mary it was their detestation of the pope, their detestation indeed of any form of foreign control in matters either religious or secular. Mary did not understand but she allowed herself to be guided and her first steps in her religious policy were cautious and careful. She encouraged the revival of the old religious services but she did not forbid the new ones. She deprived the reformers among her bishops and restored good Catholics like Gardiner of Winchester and Bonner of London to their sees. A few of the most vigorous exponents of the new faith, like Hooper and Ridley and Latimer and Cranmer, she imprisoned on one pretext or another. Against Cranmer, of course, she could charge high treason. He had been one of Lady Jane's most active supporters. Cranmer indeed had many sins to answer for. In the creation of the Edwardine liturgy and the formulation of the Edwardine articles of faith he had been the head and front of the offending. And more remotely, but even more vividly, in Mary's memory he had given the sanction of the church to the putting away of her mother by her father. But except for Cranmer and a few others Mary encouraged those who could not reconcile themselves to the Catholic order to depart in peace. The foreign Protestant divines all fled away to Switzerland and the Rhine land, practically un-heeded, and many of the more zealous English Protestants followed after them to set up nursery schools in Basel and Frankfort and Geneva for the Puritanism which was to come. Even Hugh Lat-imer, the bravest and most eloquent of them all, might have got away had he been other than the man he was.

Before Mary had been on the throne a month mass was being said all over England and the more ardent of the "hot gospelers" had been reduced to silence. She was ready to apply the detested royal supremacy that far. Further than that she did not go, awaiting the action of parliament. It is a striking testimony to the validity of her father's handiwork that Mary saw the necessity of gaining for any fundamental change in her religious ar-rangements statutory support, even though she would have been the last to admit that matters religious were subject to political control.

Parliament met in October 1553. There is little evidence of any attempt on Mary's part to influ-ence the elections. The legislation enacted may fairly be taken to reflect the sentiments of the nation at large. It annulled Queen Katherine's divorce and established Mary's legitimacy, it repealed all the ecclesiastical legislation of Edward's reign and restored the conditions of Henry VIII's last years. But it would go no further. It definitely would not rescind the royal supremacy and it definitely refused to entertain any proposal for the restoration of church lands.

Next to religion the question foremost in the minds of the English was the queen's marriage. The whole notion of a woman monarch was quite new and strange to English experience. They were sure that she should marry and they were, with very few exceptions, insistent that she should marry an Englishman. It was inevitably assumed that her husband, whoever he was, would dominate her policy and if he were a foreigner would subordinate English interests to those of his own country. As between foreigners, with Valois and Habsburg as the obvious alternatives, the English leaned traditionally towards the Habsburgs who represented the old Burgundian connection and controlled the chief continental market for English commodities. But the Habsburgs were many things, German and Spanish as well as Flemish. For the moment they were predominantly Spanish. England had nothing in common with Spain, no interests to be served by closer connection with

Spain and a good many interests to be jeopardized if she were drawn into the complicated imperial intrigues which now centered in Spain. Yet Mary, as we have seen, leaned strongly towards Spain. And Spain had in Philip II a bridegroom ready, some ten years younger than Mary to be sure and already affianced to a Portuguese princess, but still eligible. Charles V was prepared to concede almost anything to bring the match to pass and Mary favored it herself. Here again her disposition ran definitely counter to the wishes of her people.

Stephen Gardiner, the lord chancellor, would have preferred a match with Edward Courtney, earl of Devon, who had royal blood in his veins, but Courtney's private life was such as to make him totally unfit. Others spoke of Reginald Pole, also of royal lineage, who had been long overseas, was a cardinal of the church and apparently indisposed to marriage. No other domestic suitors were considered. Others could no doubt have been found if time had served, but by the end of October 1553 Mary had already made her commitments. She had told Renard, the imperial ambassador, that she meant to give her hand to Philip II.

For some months she and Renard kept her decision secret and meanwhile every effort was made to divert her from her known inclinations. Gardiner continued to work hard for Courtney, the French ambassador moved heaven and earth to prevent a Spanish marriage, the house of commons definitely petitioned the queen to take an English husband. But by the end of the year all parties had resigned themselves to the inevitable and early in January 1554 imperial plenipotentiaries arrived in England to draw up the marriage treaty. The terms agreed upon were favorable enough. Mary was to get a marriage jointure of £60,000 a year for life; she was not to be taken abroad without her consent, nor her children taken without the consent of parliament; and no foreigners were to be admitted to positions in the royal household or the navy or the army, and the English fleet was not to be removed to any foreign port, and Philip's connection with England, should Mary die childless, was to end at her death. No doubt the terms were favorable. The emperor showed himself ready and eager to concede any reasonable demand. But that did not make the impending marriage popular or even acceptable to the English. Already before the formal negotiations had begun a group of conspirators had met in London and had laid plans for a general rebellion. The plot contemplated simultaneous uprisings in the southwest, in Wales, in Warwickshire and in Kent. Gardiner got wind of it in advance and managed to prevent it in the west and in the midlands. But it presently assumed dangerous proportions in Kent. There it was led by Sir Thomas Wyatt, the son of the poet and a bold and skillful leader. He gathered a considerable force together at Rochester. Wyatt's professed objective was to prevent the Spanish marriage. He held out promise also of a restoration of Protestantism but it is significant that he placed the issue of a foreign marriage first.

The privy council seemed powerless to cope with the situation. Mary had no troops and found it difficult to raise any. She induced the city of London to supply her with 500 men whom she dispatched into Kent under the duke of Norfolk. They had no sooner come into sight of Wyatt's forces than they went over to the rebels *en masse* and Norfolk only saved himself by hard riding.

The situation looked grave indeed. Probably at no time under the Tudors had it looked graver. There was no army at all to interpose when Wyatt took up his march towards London. Had he moved promptly he might very well have achieved his purpose. But while he lingered on the way Mary herself, more resolute than all her councilors, went down in person to the London guild-hall and made a stirring appeal to the loyalty of her subjects. So it was that when Wyatt reached Southwark and would have crossed London Bridge to the city, he found the gate closed, the drawbridge up and thousands of citizens in arms to oppose him. He tried another approach from the west and actually penetrated into London as far as Ludgate before he was stopped. At that point, with his retreat cut off, he had to surrender. Perhaps he had been foolhardy to attempt alone what had really been planned as only one part of a concerted uprising, to be supported by armed assistance from France. Even so he came perilously near succeeding. What he had counted on was a spontaneous outbreak of the Londoners in his favor; failing that he had no chance. One can hardly resist the conclusion that it was Mary's own resolution and her eloquent appeal to the Londoners that had saved the day and perhaps the throne. It was the sort of thing Henry VIII or Elizabeth could have done and it reveals potentialities in Mary which might have made her a great leader of her people had she not been preoccupied with a foreign church and a foreign husband. It reveals also how completely the Tudor monarchs were dependent upon popular support when a resolute man with no more than 4,000 followers at his heels could come so near to overthrowing them when they took the unpopular side.

Wyatt's attempt and failure changed the whole character of Mary's rule. Had she been wiser it might have served as a solemn warning. As it was her success simply strengthened her resolution to persist in the course she had defined for herself and to deal resolutely and ruthlessly with those who opposed it. Her first blow was struck at two innocent victims in the Tower, already adjudged guilty of high treason, Lady Jane Grey and her husband, Guilford Dudley. They had not in any way been implicated in the Wyatt uprising and could hardly have hoped to profit by it even if it had been successful. But they were marked to die, Dudley first and after him Jane. Jane was just past sixteen, a lovely young woman with all the graces of mind and body. She met death very bravely, loyal to the last to the faith she cherished. Her contribution to English history was the revelation of a beautiful, devoted, unselfish Christian spirit under circumstances in which the mainsprings of human action are almost certain to be revealed.

Other executions followed rapidly, Suffolk, Jane's father, Lord Thomas Grey, her uncle, both of them directly implicated in Wyatt's attempt, and Wyatt himself, of course. And there were wholesale hangings of the rank and file, on the London gates, in the London streets and scattered through the Kentish villages. This was customary and except in the case of Lady Jane aroused no popular sympathy.

Mary's more difficult problem was that of dealing with her half-sister Elizabeth. Wyatt, before his death, is said to have made statements damaging to her innocence and Courtney admitted that there had been some talk of marriage for him with her. Whether these stories were true or not there can be no doubt that the rebels regarded Elizabeth as of their party. Mary herself was for getting rid of her and the imperial ambassador did all he could to bring about her trial and execution. But Gardiner apparently opposed that course though he favored debarring her from the succession. The truth of the matter was that they had not the shadow of a case against Elizabeth. Even Wyatt exonerated her on the scaffold. She was put in the Tower for a time and later sent to Woodstock, where she remained virtually a prisoner for the better part of a year. After that she was gradually received back into favor and spent the rest of Mary's reign sometimes at court, sometimes at Hatfield, her favorite residence. Mary never trusted her but Elizabeth's conduct was impeccable. Philip befriended her later, particularly after it became apparent that Mary would be childless, on the grounds that Spain would be better off with Elizabeth on the English throne than with the only probable alternative, the Frenchified Mary Stuart.

With Wyatt out of the way, Mary called her parliament and laid before it the terms of her marriage treaty for ratification. On the wave of popular enthusiasm following the suppression of the rebellion the bill passed unopposed. London did not like it much and continued to express its anti-Spanish sentiments in rather ribald poems but England at large was at least acquiescent. In July Philip landed at Southampton and four days later married Mary in Winchester Cathedral. And so Mary achieved what was perhaps her most cherished purpose.

That done, the way was cleared for the restoration of England to the fold of the old church. So far nothing much more had been done than to sweep away the Edwardine legislation. Altars had been set up, the mass reëstablished and a great many of the clergy had been ejected from their livings. But England was still a long way from Rome. The business of leading her back was entrusted to Reginald Pole, cardinal and papal legate, who had been dispatched by the pope to England immediately after Mary's accession but had been detained in Flanders by the emperor lest his zealous Romanism, during the period when Mary was getting herself established, would do more harm than good. Pole finally landed in England towards the end of November 1554. Parliament was already in session. Pole appeared before it on the 28th of the month and on the following day both houses joined in a petition to be reunited to the Roman communion. On the very last day of the month Pole pronounced national absolution from the sin of schism. After appropriate rejoicings parliament settled down to the business of enacting the necessary legislation. All the statutes passed against Rome since 1528 were repealed and the old heresy laws were reënacted. But the church lands were not restored. This was made clear by statute, it was made clear by papal dispensation; to make assurance doubly sure papal dispensation was actually embodied in act of parliament. And so England went back to the Roman fold, the prodigal returned with all his ill-gotten gains safely buttoned in his pockets. Mary liked to believe it was an act of faith, a conversion *en masse*. No doubt for a few it was, but for the great majority of the English it was obedience to the law. The same men and women went to mass and told their beads who had a few years before accepted the second prayer-book and who were a few years later to accept Elizabethan Anglicanism. Even among the parish clergy at least three-quarters accepted the Catholic order, even among the bishops a substantial minority carried over. The official church was after all the queen's business; let her look to it if it was not according to the divine purpose. Unless we grasp this point of view and realize how prevalent it was we shall never understand how it came to pass that the English in thirty years accepted five distinct changes in their religion without any great fuss about the matter.

But conformity there must be. Hardly anyone in the sixteenth century doubted that. Religious dissent was no more to be tolerated than political rebellion. The parliament which reënacted the heresy laws, while it turned over the definition of heresy to the church, placed at the disposal of the church the full strength of the temporal arm. We need not conclude that parliament contemplated any wholesale application of the heresy laws. There was always in Tudor times a deep gulf fixed between the enactment of legislation and its enforcement. But parliament in any case supplied the machinery. It was the church courts, stimulated by the royal zeal, that applied it. Mary herself, in the last analysis, was responsible for the fires of Smithfield.

Active religious persecution began in January 1555 and continued without any marked interruption for the rest of the reign. John Foxe, in his so-called *Book of Martyrs*, told the story in detail a few years afterwards, with a venomous bias to be sure but with a respect for facts which entitles him to a high place among honest historians. The victims were drawn from both sexes and from all classes. Of them all the most conspicuous were Ridley and Latimer, who were burned in Oxford in October 1555, and Cranmer himself, who suffered the following spring. Ridley and Latimer died side by side, Latimer being then past seventy. His last words furnish the keynote to a long life devoted to the service of his God. "Be of good comfort, Master Ridley," he shouted above the crackling of the flames, "we shall this day light such a candle by God's grace in England as I trust shall never be put out."

Cranmer was not so stout-hearted; he was perhaps not so sure. His was the type of mind which sees the other side of every question. After his trial and condemnation for heresy he signed no less than seven recantations. They did not save him. They served rather the purpose of his enemies, or would have had he persisted in the denial of his faith to the end. But he disappointed expectations and in his last speech before execution he spoke out bravely for the faith he had done so much to define and enrich. When the fires were lighted he held the hand which had signed the recantations first to the flames.

Altogether something like three hundred were burned for heresy. Most of the executions were in London and the eastern and southern counties, the traditional strongholds of Protestant dissent. The number of those who suffered seems ridiculously small as compared with contemporary holocausts on the continent. But it was large for England, in fact it was unique for England. On that account it created a pattern of Rome and the ways of Rome on the English mind which three centuries have not been able to eradicate.

So far as Mary's religious purposes were concerned, her persecution of the heretics did more harm than good. And it increased her unpopularity, already badly damaged by her Spanish marriage. It was her particular misfortune that the two things in the world to which she was most devoted, her husband and her religion, were the two things which most estranged her from her people.

To make matters worse she bore Philip no children.

The wisest of her councilors, Stephen Gardiner, died in 1555. He was a patriotic Englishman and he did much to keep Mary alive to her national responsibilities. After his death she fell increasingly under the influence of her husband and of Cardinal Pole, neither of whom understood or cared much about English problems and English interests. And presently Mary's subjects came to realize that it was of Spain she was thinking and Rome, not England. The consequence was that she found it increasingly difficult to get on with her parliaments, notwithstanding the fact that she made every effort to pack them with her supporters. They would not disinherit her sister, they would not return the confiscated church property, they would not agree to the coronation of her husband. They did not give her enough money for her purposes and compelled her to resort to forced loans. And there was nothing Philip could do, though he tried hard enough, to overcome the national distrust of him and his purposes. His liberality was construed as bribery, his efforts to build up the English navy as a shrewd stroke for Spain. It was remarked that he did nothing to open the doors of his colonial empire to English traders. During the last two years of the reign a whole series of plots developed to rid the land of the Spanish incubus. Most of them were hatched in Paris and none of them assumed serious proportions but they are indicative of the drift of sentiment.

No doubt Philip II tried to exploit the strength of England for his own purposes. He was pledged by the marriage treaty not to disturb England's relations with her neighbors but no treaty could limit his influence over his doting wife. Mary was eager to follow where he beckoned and so it was that in 1557 he drew her into a war against France. The initial engagements were favorable to the Anglo-Spanish forces but they simply served to lull the English into a false sense of security. They had one stronghold in France, Calais, the last remnant of their fourteenth century conquests. It was a source of weakness rather than strength but it was a great source of national pride. For two hundred and eleven years it had been in English hands. Its fortifications had been allowed to fall into decay and its garrison was sadly depleted. The consequence was that when the French made a sudden descent upon it in January 1558 it was not strong enough to resist. It surrendered after a week's siege. Philip did nothing to save it and he made no effort to recover it. So far as England was concerned its fall marked the end of the war. It marked also the end of Philip's influence in English affairs, and it broke Mary's heart.

The rest of her life is without significance. She still hoped that her husband would come back to her and she still hoped for a baby, but she hoped in vain. The war petered out in August with Calais in French hands. Parliament sat and rose again without any definite achievement except to furnish inadequate funds for an unpopular war. But no more could fairly have been expected of it. The initiative in legislation still lay with the crown and the crown consisted of a distracted woman and a group of privy councilors too busy quarreling among themselves to concert any forward-looking policy. One gets the impression, during the closing months of Mary's life, of a government and a nation apathetic, dispirited, without purpose, almost without hope.

After June 1558 England was pretty plainly simply waiting for the queen to die and was casting its eyes anxiously towards Elizabeth, the rather enigmatical young woman at Hatfield house. Mary was a moderately long time adying but she died at last in November, conscious at the last

chiefly of her failures. They would find the word
Calais, she said, written upon her heart.

It is not easy to form a just estimate of her or of
her reign. What she had tried to do, that she had,
superficially at least, done. She had brought England back to the Roman fold, she had wiped away
the stain upon her mother's memory and she had
married the greatest prince in Christendom. But
she had not won the love of her husband and she
had not brought a child into the world. As a wife
and a mother she had failed. And she had not won
the hearts of her people and she had not really
converted them to Roman Catholicism. Nothing in
fact that Mary had done had any permanence. The
Roman church and the Spanish alliance both
passed with her passing and the woman who succeeded her embodied in her own person all the
things she had fought against. For England and in
the development of England Mary's reign was a
barren interlude, alike barren in law and in politics,
in economic and social progress, in art and in letters. It is hard to realize that the nation was about
to enter perhaps the most glorious period in its
history. Certainly that glory was not of Mary's
making. It was those things which she had abased
that were to be exalted and those stones which she
had rejected that were to be the head of the corner.

ELIZABETH

CHAPTER V

ELIZABETH

T IS hard to get at the truth about Queen Elizabeth. She has become one of the articles of the English national faith, and good Englishmen from John Hayward to John Neale have conspired together to glorify her. This much at least is certain, that she was the all-important person in the England of her time, and her personality probably the most influential single factor in shaping the history of it. Without Elizabeth many things might have happened, but certainly not Elizabethan England.

At the time of her accession she was five and twenty—a fine figure of a woman, rather tall, well poised, with an olive complexion, singularly alert eyes and reddish-golden hair. She took care that you should notice her shapely hands and feet. Strength and pride were the dominating notes in her countenance. It lacked warmth and what we should call nowadays feminine charm. Evidently she was wise in the ways of the world and com-

[145]

petent to cope with them. She had been reared in a hard school. Her mother had been executed before she was three, and for most of her early girlhood she had lived under the stigma of bastardy. During her brother's reign she had been drawn into an unsavory affair with Lord Admiral Seymour, and under her sister had been the focal point of virtually every conspiracy against the crown. Mary would gladly have executed her for high treason had she been able to produce any convincing evidence against her. Her escape was in any case something of a miracle. In short, Elizabeth grew up in an atmosphere of intrigue and suspicion and distrust, with dangerous enemies and even more dangerous friends all about her. It was not a happy girlhood, not one calculated to develop the more lovable womanly qualities. But it was a fine training for statescraft. No wonder if, at five and twenty, she was resourceful, self-reliant, a keen judge of men and their motives, a practical politician of the first water.

She had need of exceptional endowments to face the problems that confronted her. England was still at war with France and Calais still in the hands of the enemy. Peace negotiations, to be sure, were in progress but they were not making rapid headway. Elizabeth had an uneasy feeling that given the opportunity, her Spanish ally might leave her in the lurch. It was pretty evident also that the French were seriously contemplating a renewal of hostilities along the Scottish border. The national treasury was empty and the English crown was in debt to Antwerp bankers for something like a quarter of a million pounds. Trade was almost at a standstill, English money was debased and English credit in a bad way. The English people had lost confidence in their government and were glancing this way and that, uneasily about, like sheep without a shepherd.

The most serious problem of all was that of religion. With Mary's death the burnings of heretics had ceased, but otherwise the situation remained unchanged, except for the fact that Cardinal Pole's death which followed hard upon Mary's had left the church in England without a primate. England was still part of the Roman communion, the same communion which had branded the young woman now on the English throne as a bastard.

Elizabeth proceeded with care and deliberation. In changing her government she retained eleven of Mary's counselors and added only seven new ones. But the new ones were the ones that mattered, most of all Sir William Cecil and his brother-in-law, Sir Nicholas Bacon. Cecil was to be her chief counselor for forty years to come. Already, although he was not yet forty, he was an experienced statesman. He had been secretary under Somerset and again under Northumberland, and though he barely escaped implication in the Lady Jane Grey conspiracy, he had been seriously considered for the same office under Mary. We should certainly regard this record as an eloquent testimony to Cecil's competency. It was hardly a less eloquent testimony to his adaptability. He was, by choice, a Protestant but he was an Englishman first and a Protestant afterwards.

The French would have called him a *politique*. He was of course a commoner, one of the new gentry who had fattened on the spoils of the church. Bacon conformed in the main to the same type and so did most of Elizabeth's trusted advisers. But from the start she liked to keep a balance between faction and faction and although her choice of Cecil was significant, men found it difficult to judge from the complexion of her council whether she meant to hunt with the Radicals or the Conservatives, the Catholics or the Protestants.

With only a few faint gestures of disapproval at the existing arrangements, she deferred the settlement of religion until the meeting of her first parliament. Meanwhile, she stopped preaching in all camps. This merely postponed the decision; it did not in any real sense relieve her of the responsibility of it. Parliament might ratify or it might not ratify, or it might amend, but she must initiate. It was a difficult decision, the more difficult because she had few convictions on the subject herself. She was committed by the facts of her birth to the break from Rome, but she had been well-schooled by the circumstances of her upbringing to accept whatever religion the government imposed. A Henrican Catholic during her father's lifetime, she had become first a moderate and then a rather radical Protestant under her brother and then, with as good a grace as might be, a Roman Catholic at her sister's bidding. She seems to have accepted all these changes without difficulty and without any emotional disturbance. Notwithstanding the valiant attempts of Protestant historians to figure her forth as a champion of the faith, there can be little doubt that she was at heart profoundly secular. And she was English to the bone, with less foreign blood in her veins than any English sovereign since the Danish conquest. In both of these respects she stood in sharp contrast to her sister.

Being the strong nationalist that she was, Elizabeth was bound to accept the break from Rome as a fundamental condition for her religious establishment. And she was well assured that the great majority of her subjects, Catholic as well as Protestant, leaned strongly towards an independent national church. But the foreign situation presented serious difficulties. Her one European ally, Philip of Spain, was an ardent Catholic and almost certain to be alienated by any indication of heretical tendencies on her part. Failing him, the only alternative was France. But France was definitely committed to the English claims of Mary Queen of Scots, whose orthodoxy was beyond question and whose title to the English throne was, in Catholic eyes, considerably better than her own. As for the European Protestant states, their fighting strength was negligible even if they had been united, instead of being split up as they were into hostile camps of Lutheran and Calvinist. Protestantism indeed was a good deal weaker than it had been, and Roman Catholicism, purified by the Council of Trent, a good deal stronger. Elizabeth herself was disposed to discount the force of religion in international politics. She had observed her father and her brother carry through their revolutionary ecclesiastical changes without any serious disturbance of their foreign relations. But not many people were of her way of thinking. The fear of a Holy War, of a united crusade of Catholic Europe against heresy, was a very lively fear in her time, and constituted a strong argument against religious change.

Elizabeth's first parliament met in January. It seems to have been elected without royal interference and it may be taken to represent a fair cross-section of national sentiment. It established royal supremacy over the English church as it had been under Henry VIII and it imposed upon England a uniform church service, forbidding any other kind of service and imposing light fines upon laymen who did not attend the established one. The service imposed was, with one significant exception, that of Edward VI's Second Prayer Book. The exception was that in the ritual of the communion service two sentences were added which seemed to admit the Real Presence in the sacrament, although the sentence was retained which emphasized its purely commemorative character. This may have been done to conciliate the Lutheran princes or to appease the English Catholics. In any case it serves to illustrate the spirit of compromise which characterized the Elizabethan religious settlement.

What emerged was a national church under the queen, with a church service imposed by parliament and a personnel nominated by the Crown. It was a definite and complete subordination of church to state. So far as the church government was concerned it retained the old Catholic hierarchy of archbishops, bishops, deacons, priests, and the rest, and the old methods of selecting them. It made little change in ecclesiastical vestments or church ornaments. Its prayer book was fundamentally a translation of the Catholic service books. So far it was distinctly conservative. Its concessions to the radicals were in dogma rather than ritual, and in the direction of Zwinglianism and Calvinism rather than Lutheranism. But Elizabeth insisted that her church was mere English and in the whole course of her public policy she kept free from entangling commitments to European Protestants of any complexion.

The actual installation of the new establishment naturally presented considerable difficulties and involved very considerable changes in church personnel, particularly in the upper ranks. In the summer and autumn of 1559 all the Marian bishops were gradually unseated and others, nearly all of them Marian exiles, saturated with Zwinglian ideas, were appointed in their stead. It is to be noted that although the deprived bishops were placed under restraint they were seldom sent to the Tower and never to the block. As for the rank and file of the clergy, probably not ten per cent of them lost their preferments. The settlement was imposed with amazingly little friction and almost no persecution. It forbade liberty of worship, but there was no inquisition, no opening of windows into men's souls. And there can be little doubt that it did accomplish what Elizabeth intended. It secured the support of the great majority of the English, if without enthusiasm, certainly without protest. There were those, of course, who stood valiantly for the old faith but they were a small and a diminishing minority. During the first decade of the reign, Roman Catholicism steadily lost ground in England and had Elizabeth been able to work out her problem according to her original plan without foreign interference, the story of religious persecution in her reign might well have been a blank page.

Unfortunately this was not to be. Religion was too much entangled in politics. Elizabeth was wise enough to realize that however she might view the matter, her decision on the religious question would influence profoundly her relation with her neighbors. It did not follow that it would be the determining factor, but it inevitably would predispose the Protestant powers in her favor and the

Catholic powers against her. In the case of France and Spain, the two neighbors from which she had most to fear, Spain was of course her ally and the king of Spain her brother-in-law, France was her enemy and was formally committed to the English pretensions of Mary Stuart. Spain and France were at the moment at war. For over half a century they had been for most of the time at war, and it was a fair presumption that the political and dynastic considerations which had so often divided them would effectually prevent any close coöperation between them. But they were the chief pillars of the Roman church, and the Roman church had recovered from the first shock of the Reformation movement, had done much to set its house in order and was calling upon Catholic christendom to unite and destroy the enemies of the faith. Would France and Spain respond? Elizabeth thought not. Philip II revealed every disposition to continue his English connection. He even went so far as to propose marriage to Elizabeth and when she declined, directed his ambassador to assure her that it would make no difference to their friendship. And yet within a year Philip had taken a French wife. Marriage among the Habsburgs was the usual preliminary to political alliance.

As for France, the most important factor in the

determination of her policy toward England at the moment was the claim of Mary Stuart to the English throne. The French king had already proclaimed her English title and she had already quartered the English arms with those of France and Scotland on her coat-of-arms. Her uncles of Guise were very influential at the French court. Her mother of Guise was governing Scotland virtually as a French province. It was greatly to be feared that as soon as France got free from her war with Spain she would concentrate her energies on England. And when peace did come it brought, by an untimely accident at the peace celebrations in Paris, the death of Henry II and the accession of Mary Stuart's husband, Francis II, to the French throne. The Guises were at once in the saddle and there could not be the slightest doubt about their malevolence toward Elizabeth. The question was not what they wanted to do but whether they could do it. And the answer to that question depended upon many things. It depended upon their ability to maintain their dominating position in French politics. There were many other powerful families in France disposed to question that, and there was at least one resolute woman in France, a clever, resourceful, unscrupulous Italian woman, Catherine de Medici, the queen mother, very much disposed to question it. And there were also the French Protestants, the Huguenots, still a proscribed sect but rapidly growing in numbers and rapidly perfecting a fighting organization, who saw in the Guises the great enemies of their faith. The Guises, strong as they were, were by no means assured of a united France behind them and they could not count upon Spain's support in a policy designed to lead the British Isles in captivity to France. Philip II was an ardent Catholic and a hater of heretics, if anyone was, but the notion of assisting the Valois to annex England or even of remaining benevolently neutral while that was taking place, violated all the fundamental principles of Habsburg international policy. Elizabeth could pretty certainly count upon assistance both within France and without France to meet the Guisan menace.

Immediately, the focal point of the matters at issue between England and France was in Scotland. When Elizabeth came to the throne, Mary of Guise was still governing Scotland as regent for her daughter, Mary Stuart, and was converting Scotland as quickly as might be into a French dependency. In consequence, she was arousing in that disordered country a spirit of hostility toward France, which was rapidly displacing its inveterate hostility toward England. The fear of absorption by England had driven the Scots into the arms of France originally; the Scottish policy of Henry VIII and after him of the Protector Somerset, had served to quicken rather than to allay that fear; the French marriage of Mary Queen of Scots, and her education in France had been the supreme expression of it. But the Scotch had no notion of jumping from the frying pan into the fire and as the French intentions became increasingly apparent a strong nationalistic, anti-French sentiment took form. It was fed by the growth of Protestantism, which notwithstanding the efforts of the government spread rapidly through the north. There were other elements in the Scottish situation as well, personal rivalries and clan rivalries, and hungry acquisitive instincts for which the Scotch were even then notorious; but from Elizabeth's point of view the promising elements were the anti-French sentiment and the Protestant sentiment. For to a Scotland, anti-French and Protestant, England was the obvious friend, in fact the indispensable friend. John Knox was the prophet of this new Scotland, and the Lords of the Congregation, a group of Protestant nobles banded together by a covenant, the operating organization. Elizabeth had not been on the throne many

months before the issue was definitely joined and
Mary of Guise and the Lords of the Congregation
were at war. The war went badly for the Protestants and it soon became evident that unless aid
were forthcoming from England they could hardly
expect to rid themselves of French control. The
Lords appealed to Elizabeth and she was faced
with the disagreeable alternatives of either helping
rebels against their anointed sovereign or else of
losing a very promising opportunity to secure her
back door against the old French enemy. It was
characteristic of her and was to be characteristic of
her policy throughout her reign that she undertook to help her rebellious Scottish friends without seeming to help them. She sent them money
and munitions of war underhand. But by the end
of the year 1559 it appeared that secret help was
not enough. Elizabeth had therefore in the end
to intervene openly, sending first a fleet to the
Forth to block reinforcements from France and
then an army to drive the French out of Leith.
And so she induced them to come to terms and by
the Treaty of Edinburgh in 1560 secured a peace
in the north which sent them apacking and left
the Protestant, pro-English Lords of the Congregation supreme.

It was a great achievement and it proved to be

a permanent one. Throughout the rest of Elizabeth's reign England and Scotland were not only at peace, but in close alliance. The French attempted more than once to recover their foothold in the north but they never came dangerously near to succeeding. The significance of the Treaty of Edinburgh lies not so much in the fact that it was a victory for England over France as that it was a victory for Protestantism over Catholicism. It did, in short, establish the Protestant supremacy permanently in Scotland and the Protestant supremacy meant inevitably an English alliance. Elizabeth was content with that much. She cherished no imperial designs on Scotland and wished to have no more to do with that country than was necessary to keep it faithful to its English commitments. Her Scottish friends would have welcomed large pensions and would gladly have drawn her actively into their domestic broils but she kept her distance and achieved her purpose. During her reign, Scotland and England, after centuries of inveterate hostility, got used to being at peace, and Scotland learned from her that England had no designs upon her independence. And so it came to pass that after her death, with a minimum amount of friction and difficulty, the two countries came together under a common sovereign.

At one time in the course of Elizabeth's consideration of the Scotch problem, it had been suggested that she marry the earl of Arran, who had a good claim to the Scotch throne in case Mary Stuart should die without offspring. The matter never came to anything, hardly even to the preliminaries of a courtship, but it serves to disclose the fact that the question of Elizabeth's marriage was an inevitable concomitant of any diplomatic affair to which she was a party. Everyone believed that she would marry. No one supposed that she had courage and self-reliance sufficient to face the problems of monarchy without a husband's assistance and no one imagined that she could resist the primitive urge to wifehood and motherhood. Her subjects, even her intimate counselors, believed it to be essential that she should marry. As they saw it, the security of the state and of the Protestant religion rested upon the establishment of the succession in the heirs of her body. But the selection of the bridegroom was a difficult matter. He must either be an Englishman or a foreigner. There seemed to be no eligible Englishman of befitting rank available, and a foreigner meant, as they bitterly recalled from Mary's reign, foreign entanglements. With a French or a Spanish or an Imperial bridegroom, and princely candidates from all three countries were offered, the question of religion got involved. Was it safe to expose English Protestantism to the dangerous, insidious influence of a Roman Catholic prince consort? They thought not. What the queen thought was not easily apparent. Sometimes she said that she meant to live and die a virgin, sometimes that assuredly she would marry, sometimes that she was ready to marry if her own inclinations prompted it or the welfare of her kingdom necessitated it. The probabilities are that she lacked strong sex impulse though there is no sound reason for believing that she was incapable of bearing children. At the outset of her reign she was beset with suitors who included among their number the king of Spain, the heir apparent to the Swedish throne, two of the younger sons of the German emperor, and the earl of Arran. To this number the king of France and two of his brothers were later to be added, and perhaps Henry of Navarre. It was a formidable list and she listened to them all, and flirted with them all, and ultimately rejected them all. So far as these foreign courtships were in question it is pretty clear that Elizabeth's affections, if she had any, were never engaged. She discovered early that there were solid diplomatic advantages accruing from her unmarried state and she exploited them for all they might be worth. That was perhaps one reason why she never did marry. A foreign marriage or indeed any marriage would almost certainly have involved commitments which would have more or less restricted her freedom of action in the diplomatic game she loved to play. For not to be married always left the door open to the possibilities of marriage, and that was an asset of first rate importance which she did not care to lose.

Besides her foreign suitors, she had her domestic favorites, we can hardly call them suitors, with whom she was apparently on some sort of an emotional footing, notably Robert Dudley, earl of Leicester, Sir Christopher Hatton, and at the very end of her life, the young earl of Essex. Of these, Dudley alone seriously aspired to her hand and in the first year or two of her reign it looked very much as though she would marry him. He was married at the time, but his wife, Amy Robsart, managed to fall downstairs and break her neck very opportunely. It was probably suicide but it looked like murder. Opinions differ as to whether Elizabeth loved Dudley or not and as to whether her decision not to marry him represented a concession to a public opinion definitely opposed to the marriage, or an inadequate emotional commitment on her part. In any case, she did abandon the idea. Leicester remained close beside her during all the rest of his life and played a part in the shaping of her policy which was probably out of proportion to his merits, but she never again seriously considered him as a consort.

There can be little doubt that Elizabeth's marriage, with the dependent question of the succession, was the matter uppermost in the minds of her subjects during the first decade of her reign. In the parliament which met in 1563 and again in 1566 it was the chief item of business and it came near to opening a dangerous breach between her and her council. She was left in no doubt at all about popular sentiment on the subject, but she managed to avoid a definite commitment. Indeed her chief concern during this first decade was to avoid definite commitments in any direction. Notwithstanding her ecclesiastical arrangements she contrived to convey the impression that she was still undecided on the religion question and so to keep the good will of Philip II and to stave off hostile action by the pope. She permitted the clergy in convocation to define the faith in thirty-nine articles, but she definitely prevented their ratification by parliament. Her one great mistake was in her relations with France. The outbreak of the first religious war in that country in 1562 misled her into believing that active interference in support of the anti-Guisan faction might result in establishing a government there friendly to herself and friendly to Protestantism. She even dreamed of recovering Calais and perhaps some part of the lost Lancastrian dominions in Normandy and Guienne. In any case after the expenditure of a considerable amount of blood and treasure she failed, and when the warring factions in France had composed their differences, they joined together to drive the English forces out of the country. It was an expensive lesson but a valuable one. Thereafter she very definitely abandoned Lancastrian dreams and she abandoned as well inherited Lancastrian animosities. We may mark in the Treaty of Troyes in 1564 which brought the French war to an end, the beginnings of a policy which without much modification was to govern her relations with that country for the rest of her reign. She recognized that there was a strong Guisan Catholic party in France steadily hostile to her and a fairly strong Huguenot party in France whose friendship she could pretty steadily count on. But she recognized also the presence of a large middle party, the *politiques,* which was neither pro-English nor anti-English, but resolutely French, and disposed to subordinate religious considerations to national ones. And she saw in Catherine de Medici, the dominating personality behind the various weakling Valois kings who occupied the French throne between 1561-89, a woman prompted by very much the same considerations as herself. Catherine plainly meant to govern France for her sons and was no more inclined to yield to the domination of the Guises than she was to yield to their opponents. She certainly was not inclined to exhaust the resources of her adopted country to feed Guisan Anglophobia.

Elizabeth therefore concluded or at least proceeded to act as though she had concluded that if France was not to be regarded as an assured friend, she was certainly not to be regarded as an assured enemy. She also concluded that if France could be kept busy with her domestic difficulties she was not likely to pursue an aggressive foreign policy of any sort. And so we get on one hand a disposition on Elizabeth's part to explore the possibilities of a French alliance, as a possible alternative to her inherited alliance with Spain, and on the other a discreet, underhand meddling in French internal broils, usually in the form of financial support to the Huguenots. As a matter of fact, France, as an active aggressive force, plays a part of little or no importance in international affairs during almost the whole of Elizabeth's reign. Whether she foresaw this or not, it was certainly well that she escaped early from Lancastrian preoccupations about France and adapted herself easily to conditions as they actually were. In a rapidly changing world her opportunism was a strong asset.

From her point of view the death of Francis II, Mary Stuart's husband, was very helpful for it removed her rival from the center of French affairs to the relatively obscure position of queen dowager. Her uncles of Guise lost almost at once their dominating position in French politics and Catherine de Medici took the helm. The danger of active intervention by France in behalf of Mary's English claims or even of her Scotch prerogatives faded away. Mary found herself more or less bereft of three kingdoms almost overnight. After a futile attempt to arrange a marriage with Don Carlos, the imbecilic son of Philip II, and with Charles IX, the new king of France, she decided to return to what was left of her Scotch kingdom and in the midsummer of 1561 she took ship for the north.

It will not be possible to follow in detail the

history of her brief reign in Scotland. She found the Protestants in command and adapted herself with as good a grace as might be to their government. But she never addressed herself whole-heartedly to the business of establishing a place for herself in Scotland. The concessions which she made there to the *status quo* were simply subterfuges until she got firmly seated in the saddle. She never really contemplated the eventuality of a Protestant régime and was as well assured of a return to Roman Catholicism as John Knox was assured of the contrary. The possibility of any middle course, of any such astute blurring of the edges of religious controversy as Elizabeth had managed in the south, never occurred to her. It was not so much that she preferred her faith before her kingdom, it was rather that she never realized that she was confronted with any such definite alternatives. Mary never penetrated to the actualities of the Scottish political and religious situation, never properly understood the strength of either the Protestant or the national spirit.

She really never sought to understand it. She never approached her problem in terms of Scotland. Had she been content to accept her destiny as queen of Scotland, she might have prevailed even against John Knox himself, for she was clever and resourceful. But she had been reared to a larger purpose—queen of Scotland by birth, queen of France by marriage, queen of England by right,—of the three, Scotland was the least. Fortune was against her for the moment but she could not but regard her position in Scotland simply as a stepping stone to the larger empire of her dreams. While Elizabeth was rapidly consolidating her position in England and establishing that sympathetic contact with her people which was one of her great achievements, Mary was looking about for foreign alliances, casting covetous eyes towards the English throne, quarreling with her nobles and calling down upon her· head the wrath of her preachers.

From the outset she was much concerned with the business of getting a husband. After a good deal of looking about she finally pitched upon young Henry Darnley who had himself, through his grandmother, Margaret Tudor, a good working claim to the English throne. He was a raw, conceited boy at best, but perhaps capable of better things—at least Mary permitted herself to think so—and so she married him. The fact that he was unpopular with the Scottish leaders, John Knox and the earl of Murray, and that they regarded the match as a definite commitment on Mary's part to a policy hostile to them, did not for a moment deter her. Nothing perhaps illustrates better the fundamental difference between Mary and Elizabeth than Mary's marriage with Darnley and Elizabeth's refusal to marry Dudley.

The Darnley match was Mary's undoing. He proved to be worse than useless for any public purpose unless it were that of giving Mary her only child. Instead of lending her support in her vain efforts to free herself from the domination of the Protestant lords, he became a pliant tool in their hands. The David Rizzio murder need not detain us, nor need we investigate the truth of Henry of Navarre's *bon mot*, that James her son was well called Solomon because he was the son of David. There is no evidence of misconduct between Mary and Rizzio. He was a Catholic and a foreigner and therefore damned in Scotch eyes. Certain it is that his murder at Mary's feet when she was six months gone with child aroused a fury in her which cast all political considerations to the winds. The rest follows almost inevitably. Bothwell, a loose liver if there ever was one, and a married man, won her heart. He brought at least a resolute, ruthless spirit and she yielded herself absolutely into his hands. It was as far as possible from statescraft; it was human passion, long athirst, at last satisfied. The result, as is well known, was disaster. There seems to be little reasonable doubt that Mary conspired with Bothwell to destroy her husband. One hardly needs to accept the genuineness of the Casket Letters in order to be satisfied of that. Mary's behavior after Darnley's death is sufficiently convincing. Although Bothwell's guilt was bruited openly, she not only took no steps against him but she showered him with favors. Two months later under some show of compulsion she allowed him to carry her off, and less than a month after that, Bothwell's wife having secured a divorce in the interval, Mary married him.

The sequel was civil war, with Mary and Bothwell on one side and the Lords of the Congregation on the other. The Lords won a bloodless victory at Carberry Hill, drove Bothwell out of Scotland, and led Mary back a prisoner to Edinburgh.

After Carberry, Mary's political career was at an end. Whichever way you look at it, it is a tragic story. Lacking foreign support, Mary's one chance from the start had been to throw in her lot resolutely with the only party in Scotland capable of maintaining some kind of orderly government, to wit, the Lords of the Congregation. For a time she followed that policy, but the Darnley marriage tempted her to build up a Catholic party instead. Darnley himself wrecked that plan, threw Mary emotionally out of balance, and so drew down upon her all the calamities that followed. In the end she alienated everybody that mattered. It is easy to understand and to sympathize even with the Darnley murder, even with the Bothwell marriage. But there is no sense in trying to make Mary out other than what she was. There is certainly no sense in perpetuating the Schiller tradition about her or imagining that she was an injured innocent. Elizabeth remarked when she heard of the Rizzio murder, that had it been she, she would have seized Darnley's dagger from his belt and plunged it into his heart; but had Elizabeth been Mary, there never would have been a Rizzio to be murdered. Elizabeth would have known that foreign choir singers were not of the stuff of which confidential ministers are made.

After Carberry Mary was put in prison, was forced to sign a deed of abdication, and to set up a regency for her young son. She escaped the following spring, made head once more against her enemies, suffered a second defeat, fled from the field and escaped into England. Once safe in Carlisle and having drawn breath, she appealed to Elizabeth for help against her rebellious subjects.

It was a bold move on Mary's part and it embarrassed Elizabeth not a little. She plainly would have preferred to support Mary's cause. It was not easy to do otherwise without seeming to give open countenance to rebellion. On the other hand she realized clearly enough that the Lords of the Congregation were fighting her battles and the battles of England. Mary was a sister sovereign in distress to be sure, but she was also the Roman Catholic competitor for the English throne, and her cause and her purposes constituted the chief menace to the peace and safety of Protestant England. After some hesitation Elizabeth found a way out of the dilemma which was eminently characteristic of her. She decided to sit in judgment on Mary's case, or rather, as she chose to put it, to hear what the Scottish rebels had to say in justification of their treatment of their anointed queen. She induced both parties to accept this solution of the problem by intimating to Mary that if she were proved innocent she would be restored and by intimating to the Lords of the Congregation that if Mary were proved guilty she would receive no assistance from England. And thereupon Elizabeth appointed a commission to hear and determine.

But nothing came of it one way or the other. Elizabeth decided that it would be better if noth-

ing did. The English commissioners and some of
Elizabeth's Roman Catholic counselors as well
had an opportunity to examine the very damaging
evidence against Mary, including the famous Casket Letters, but they were not allowed to proceed to a decision. The net result was that they
neither vindicated her nor justified her rebels.
What they did do was to leave Mary's personal
honor under a heavy cloud. The Scottish lords
returned home, she remained in England in a
curiously ambiguous position somewhere between
that of a guest and that of a prisoner. For the
moment she had little or no desire to leave England, for plans were already afoot there which
seemed to her to promise a happy issue out of all
her afflictions.

The year 1569 marks one of the major crises of
Elizabeth's reign. All the elements of discontent
against her government which had been gathering
for many years and from many quarters came that
year to a head. It is perhaps safe to say that this
discontent was fundamentally with her ecclesiastical arrangements, though religion was currently
used in the sixteenth century to cover a multitude
of sins. A part of the discontent was directed
against her government, particularly against her
disposition to rely upon new men like Cecil and

Bacon and to ignore the claims of the old nobility. A part of it also was not so much anti-Elizabethan as it was anti-Tudor and reflected dissatisfaction with the whole centralizing tendencies of the Tudor régime. This was notably true north of the Trent in the lands of the Nevilles and the Percies. The situation in the north was really serious because of the strength of Roman Catholicism there, the remoteness from London, the dominance of the great houses and the state of military preparedness necessitated by the proximity of the Scottish border.

In such troubled waters Mary Stuart was quick to realize there might be good fishing. She was confirmed in her opinion by the friendly treatment she received from the northern gentry, still more definitely confirmed in it when the possibility of a marriage was suggested between her and the duke of Norfolk, the first peer in England and the leader of the conservative faction in Elizabeth's privy council.

Another favoring circumstance from Mary's point of view was the growing tension in Anglo-Spanish relations, to which there were at least three contributing causes. One of these was the slave-trading expeditions of John Hawkins to Spanish America of which there were no less than three in the 1560's. The two that were profitable provoked the wrath of Spain, the one that was disastrous provoked the wrath of England. It would take too long to go into the rights and wrongs of the matter. There was a general feeling abroad that international obligations did not extend to American waters, that there "was no peace beyond the line." Men might do things with impunity there which would have spelled war nearer home. But certainly Hawkins trespassed far and did much to exacerbate feeling between the Spanish and the English. Added to that was Philip II's cavalier treatment of Dr. Mann, the English ambassador in Spain, and to that again the affair of the Spanish pay ships. The pay ships in question, loaded with chests full of Spanish money, some £85,000 all told, put into English ports in December 1568 to escape French pirates. Elizabeth forthwith relieved them of their freight and transferred it to her treasury. She justified her action on the grounds that the money in question belonged to Italian bankers and she proceeded to arrange with them to lend it to her instead of to Spain. But this explanation did not satisfy the duke of Alva who promptly seized all English property in the Low Countries. Elizabeth retorted in kind and as luck would have it, caught consid-

erably more in her net than Alva caught in his.
The outcome was that trade between England and
the Low Countries was suspended for over three
years and the Spaniards were in a very receptive
frame of mind towards projects directed against
Elizabeth's government.

The so-called first Norfolk plot of 1569 had
therefore much potential strength—Mary herself,
Norfolk and the conservatives in the privy council, the northern Catholic earls, and in the background, Spain. With a sound plan and a resolute
leader it might have accomplished much. It certainly might have accomplished its immediate purpose which was a marriage between Norfolk and
Mary and the ejection of Cecil and his supporters
from the council. But Norfolk was not the man.
He was never sure quite what he wanted to do,
never attempted to organize his strength, and evidently hoped that somehow revolution would be
accomplished by mere murmurs of discontent. He
ought to have known Cecil better, assuredly he
ought to have known Elizabeth Tudor better. As
it was, he lost his opportunity and was lucky to
get off with a short imprisonment in the Tower.
His irresolution was the undoing of the northern
earls. They were in a mood to fight when he gave
the signal, but he never gave the signal in un-

equivocal terms, so they feinted, then withdrew, then were called to court, then in alarm took up arms before they were ready. And Spanish assistance, despite the large promises of the Spanish ambassador, was not forthcoming. Alva had his hands full at the moment with Dutch rebels, and although he might have sent regiments to assist a rebellion in being, he was not prepared to take the initiative.

There was, however, a rising in the north in the late autumn of 1569. Its supporters wore the red cross of the Crusaders on their coats and bore on their banners the five wounds of Christ. Their leaders demanded the overthrow of the Cecilians, the restoration of Mary to Scotland and the re-establishment of the old faith. To the rank and file the issue was religious, the directing impulse feudal loyalty—for the Nevilles and the Percies and the five wounds of Christ! They may have numbered at the maximum 5,000 foot and 1,200 horse. Had Scotland supported them, as they hoped, or had they been able to secure the person of Mary Stuart as they tried to do, the issue might have been different. As it was, they broke and fled before the armed forces raised to cope with them ever came within range.

And so the crisis of 1569 passed with Norfolk

in the Tower, the northern leaders refugees in Scotland, and the northern rank and file gracing the gallows in almost every village across the Trent. It served simply to establish Elizabeth a little more firmly on her throne and to demonstrate the stability of the Tudor system. Also it revealed the fact that except in the north, where many other factors were involved, English Roman Catholics, by and large, were loyal subjects. The pope was induced to believe that this was because he had not yet taken official action against their heretic queen. He proceeded to do so, and in February 1570, issued the bull *Regnans in Excelsis*, by which he excommunicated her, deprived her of her pretended right to the English throne, and absolved her subjects from their allegiance. For over ten years Elizabeth had been able to prevent it, and she had turned those years very fruitfully to the business of winning the loyalty of her subjects of all creeds. But it came at last; the issue was finally joined. Logically the English Catholics had no choice but to abandon their queen for their faith or their faith for their queen. At least so it appeared to Elizabeth's Protestant councilors. She herself was not so sure. In any event, she refused to act on the assumption that her Roman Catholic

subjects were necessarily traitors, papal bulls to
the contrary notwithstanding.

The immediate sequence of events did something to shake her confidence. For the second Norfolk plot, otherwise known as the Ridolfi plot,
trod hard on the heels of the first one. It envisaged
domestic rebellion and foreign invasion, the restoration of the old faith, the deposition of Elizabeth and the enthronement of Mary in her place,
with Norfolk as prince consort. The pope, the king
of Spain, and the duke of Alva were all involved
and an Italian merchant, Roberto Ridolfi, served
as intermediary between the English conspirators
and their foreign allies. But Cecil got wind of it
in time and by degrees learned the whole story. It
was clear enough that the duke of Norfolk, the
queen of Scotland, and the Spanish ambassador
were all deeply implicated. The Spanish ambassador was shipped out of England with scant cour-
tesy. Norfolk was executed for high treason. As
for Mary Queen of Scots, the bishop of London
expressed the general sentiment when he demanded that her head be set upon a spike on
London Bridge. Both houses of parliament joined
in petition to Elizabeth to much the same effect.
But Elizabeth thought differently and Mary was
spared, to become the focal point of conspiracy

after conspiracy in the years to come. She was not even closely confined, but was permitted to keep her state and to maintain her contacts with her friends. No doubt Elizabeth had her own good reasons for this policy although it is hard to fathom them now. Certainly it complicated not a little the problem of her advisers, and certainly she stood alone between Mary and the wrath of Protestant England in 1572, and from 1572 onward until Mary was finally brought to her reckoning.

The revelations of these critical years virtually compelled Elizabeth to reconsider her whole foreign policy. Heretofore she had been disposed to regard Spain as her friend and France as her enemy. The active participation of the Spanish ambassador in the Ridolfi plot made it quite clear that Spanish friendship was a broken reed to lean upon. A new element was introduced into the situation at this time also by the outbreak of revolt against the Spanish government in the Low Countries. The reasons for this revolt were in part economic, in part political, in part religious. Space does not serve to elaborate them. What Protestant England saw was an heroic struggle by their Dutch co-religionists against the furies of the Spanish inquisition. What the English merchants saw was

disorder and the destruction of property, a condition of things always unfavorable to business,
which went far to reconcile them with the sus-
pension of trade relations arising out of the affair
of the pay ships. What Elizabeth and her politicians saw was an opportunity to play the same
game with discontented Dutch Protestants that
Philip II had essayed to play with discontented
English Catholics. Any way you looked at it the
uprising in the Low Countries was a factor of importance in weakening the ties between England
and Spain.

On the other hand, old points at issue between
England and France were fast losing their significance. Scotland, the ancient bone of contention,
was definitely, almost irrevocably, committed to an
English alliance. Mary Stuart was a prisoner in
England and her cause had ceased to be a matter
of any moment to the French crown. And so it
came to pass by a curious reversal of what most
Englishmen had come to regard as the natural
order of things, that while Spain was plotting to
depose Elizabeth and enthrone her rival, France
showed herself quite ready to wipe out old scores
and came forward with a proposal of marriage
from Henry, duke of Anjou, the oldest brother of
the French king and the heir presumptive to the

French throne. Elizabeth, as usual, was quite ready to accept the situation as she found it. For her the rather sudden *volte face* was a mere matter of expediency. It has since been designated a diplomatic revolution.

The French marriage did not materialize—religious difficulties got in the way—but the courtship served as an agreeable medium for the establishment of amicable relations, and prepared the ground for an Anglo-French commercial treaty in the spring of 1572. If the diplomatists could have diverted the ways of trade to their own purposes, France at this juncture would have replaced the Low Countries as the distributing base for English commodities on the continent. Unfortunately it could not be done. Still more unfortunately the predominance of the party at the French court which favored an English alliance proved to be of short duration. The increasing influence over the king of its leader, Admiral Coligny, aroused the jealousy of Catherine de Medici. The fact that Coligny was a heretic placed a terrible weapon in her hands, and the gathering together of the Huguenots at Paris to celebrate the marriage of Henry of Navarre offered to her an opportunity to dispose at once not only of Coligny but also of all the other prominent leaders of his party.

And so came about the bloody massacre of St. Bartholomew's Eve. Probably the fury of the Catholic mob went much further than Catherine had intended. In any case, the massacre dealt a very damaging blow to the Anglo-French alliance. Had Catherine been a better Catholic than she was, or Elizabeth a better Protestant, it might have caused a complete breach. As it was, they both set about patching things up and before the year was out Catherine was once more suggesting the possibilities of a marriage alliance and Elizabeth once more in a mood to consider one. This time the suitor offered was the youngest brother of the French king, Francis, duke of Alençon. He was, to be sure, some twenty years younger than Elizabeth and he was short and pock-marked and ill-favored. Elizabeth herself called him her frog. But he served the purpose. Indeed the relations between England and France from St. Bartholomew's in 1572 until Alençon's death in 1584 turned chiefly about him and about the vicissitudes of his courtship.

In point of fact, Alençon occupied the important position which he did occupy in Elizabeth's calculations, not because he was heir presumptive to the French crown, but because his ambitions, which far outreached his capacities, led him at different times to put himself at the head, first of the rebellious Huguenots in France and a little later of the rebellious Dutch in the Low Countries. For Elizabeth by degrees abandoned the traditional Tudor policy of playing France against Spain and Spain against France and resorted instead to the policy of supporting Protestant rebellion in both countries. That was the real diplomatic revolution and we can date its beginning with some assurance at about the end of the year 1572, after Spain had showed her hand in the Ridolfi plot and France had wrecked the chances of an alliance with England by the St. Bartholomew's massacre. Thereafter Elizabeth's foreign policy was largely devoted to the business of feeding fires in her neighbors' houses. It was a distasteful business to her and she never entered into it whole-heartedly. She did not like encouraging rebellion; it established dangerous precedents against herself. The justification of it, if there was any justification, was the cause of the reformed religion. But she was not vitally interested in the cause of the reformed religion. Certainly she had no disposition at all to assume the rôle of Protestant champion for Europe at large. No more was she possessed by a desire for military conquests or military glory. Her one objective was the safety of England. Most of those about her held that England's only hope of safety lay in identifying herself with the Protestant cause. Elizabeth disagreed, but she was prepared to follow that course or any other course in pursuit of her objective. Her critics complain that she never gave the French Huguenots or the Dutch rebels sufficient assistance to enable them to win their fight. She was not so much interested in having them win their fight as in keeping them fighting. What we have to note in her foreign policy during the decade following 1572 is that she contributed underhand to the support of the French Protestants in every war they fought against the crown. We have to note that she lent money to the Dutch rebels, allowed English volunteers to enlist under their banners and helped them raise mercenaries in Germany. But we have to note also that when the French threatened to assist the Dutch with the idea of annexing the Low Countries she showed herself quite ready to join with the Spaniards to prevent them.

It was in this connection that Francis, duke of Alençon, came to play the part he did. For in 1576 he undertook to champion the cause of the Dutch and from that time until his death eight years later, his plans and his purpose became the most important single factor in the relations of

England, both with the Low Countries and with France. Elizabeth could never quite make up her mind about Alençon. She knew that the Dutch were courting his favor because they hoped he would bring the strength of France to their support. She knew also that Catherine de Medici wanted to get her trouble-making young son out of France at almost any price short of war. At first Elizabeth was afraid that Alençon's plans would result in the absorption of the Low Countries by France. Later she undertook to win him to her own interests by holding out vague hopes of a marriage. Later again her fear of Spain, accentuated by Philip II's annexation of Portugal in 1580, and by the successes of his new governor, Alexander of Parma, in the Low Countries, led her to the position that she had better run the risk of French aggression in the Low Countries than suffer the Spanish power to grow unchecked. All of these factors entered into her calculations and there were other factors as well which she dared not ignore. There was, as we shall see, a definite missionary effort by the Jesuits to recover England for the old faith. There was a Guisan plot on foot in Scotland to win the young Scottish king from his Protestant affiliations. There was a Spanish expedition sowing rebellion in Ireland. Elizabeth had to take account of all these things. She could not with safety retire into her insularity. The enemy was at her gates, was indeed inside her gates. What then to do with Alençon? Her main business was to place him in a position in which he could be counted upon to subserve her interests whatever those interests might turn out to be. We need not assume that she was moved by emotional considerations in the long courtship that followed, though it must be admitted that she played fast and loose with the conventions. Probably she was right in thinking that the best way to keep Alençon at her heels was to keep alive his hopes of marriage. She was, after all, despite her age, the best match in Europe and she brought a kingdom with her for a dowry. But it is more than doubtful that she really ever considered marrying him. The opposition of her Protestant subjects to the match was unmistakable and although she might storm against it and even cut off the right hand of rash pamphleteers like John Stubb who expressed it, she was too conscious of her dependence upon popular support to defy it. What came of the whole affair in the end was little or nothing. Alençon was not the man for heroic enterprises of any sort. He paid two visits to England, long outstayed his welcome on the second one and

finally had to be bribed to leave. It cost Elizabeth
£70,000 of good English money to get him away
to his Dutch campaigning. And he did rather less
than nothing for the Dutch after he reached them
It may be that she prevented him from doing a
good deal of harm and it may be that the display
of good will between France and England which
accompanied the courtship did serve as a check
upon the Spaniards. But more than that, nothing.
During the tangled negotiations there had been
talk of a definite alliance between the two countries, and there had been plans for a joint expedition to Portugal in support of Don Antonio, the
Portuguese pretender. But they never materi-
alized. Elizabeth would gladly have set France to
war against Spain, but she declined to be an effective party to the enterprise and Catherine de
Medici had no notion of engaging Spain alone.

Alençon died in the spring of 1584 and with
him died the last hope of a Valois succession. The
next in line for the French crown was young
Henry of Navarre, a heretic Huguenot. There was
matter enough in that situation to keep France engaged about her own affairs for many years to
come. So far as the Low Countries were concerned,
Alençon's death passed without notice. He had
proved himself to be a very sorry champion and

yet, while he lived, there was always the chance that he might become king of France and march in strength to their rescue. Certainly they had need of a savior. William of Orange was struggling very hard to keep their scattered forces together and to maintain an unbroken front against the enemy. He was the one leader whom the Dutch were prepared to follow and he was perhaps the only man alive who knew how to operate the complicated machinery of their government and to realize what strength there was in their loose and unstable union, and he was barely holding his own. On the thirtieth of June, 1584, he was shot at and killed by an assassin in the pay of Spain. There was no one to take his place and it seemed inevitable that the dogged patience of Philip and the consummate ability of Parma together would sweep the Dutch rebels into the sea. That was the tremendous fact which Elizabeth had to face in the midsummer of 1584. For nearly twenty years the Dutch rebels had been her first bulwark against the gathering wrath of Philip II. Once that bulwark was down, she would be face to face with the triumphant power of Spain. She might maintain a purely defensive attitude, abandon the Dutch to their almost certain fate and await attack, if there was to be an attack, behind her sea walls. Or she might take up the cudgels openly for the Dutch and force the issue with Spain at once while the ports in the Low Countries were still in the hands of her friends. One or the other of these things she must do.

But we shall not understand the bases for her decision unless we consider how events had been shaping themselves in England. Perhaps the most important fact of all was that England, for nearly twenty years, had been at peace. There had been the rising in the north, of course, and there was always endemic disorder in Ireland and along the Scottish border, but there had been nothing like a national war since the ill-advised expedition to France in 1564. It was easily the longest period of peace in Tudor history and Elizabeth had applied it to very good purpose. She had very definitely interested herself in the welfare of her people at large. At the beginning of her reign she had restored the debased coinage and had reëstablished English credit overseas. Three years later she had passed in parliament her famous Act of Apprentices which placed the whole industrial system on a national basis and under national oversight. She had undertaken to protect her peasantry from the encroachments of the enclosure movement. She had given much thought to the interests of her merchants, had extended to them preferential custom rates as against their foreign competitors, had encouraged them to seek out new ways of trade and had definitely recognized that their interests were of vital importance in her international relations. It is from her rather than from the ephemeral experiments of her predecessors that we must trace the steady development of what came to be known later as the navigation policy, or at least that part of it which meant the definite favoring of the English carriers in all English sea-borne commerce. She even went so far as to reëstablish the Catholic fish days by law in order that the English fisheries should not suffer any evil consequences from the break with Rome. She chartered companies for trade in the Baltic, in Spain, in Venice, in Turkey, on the African coast and even in the Far Indies. And she averted her eyes while John Hawkins and the likes of him stole slaves from the Guinea coast of Portugal and sold them in defiance of the Spanish embargo in the Spanish West Indies. Indeed, she is known to have invested some of her own money in their piratical enterprises. She encouraged Martin Frobisher and John Davis in their search for the northwest passage, Humphrey Gilbert and his half-brother, Walter Raleigh, in their attempts

to colonize North America, and when Francis
Drake came home in 1581 from his voyage around
the world with his little ship fairly staggering
under its cargo of Spanish silver she knighted him
on his own quarter-deck and resisted all efforts of
the Spanish king to recover any part of the enormous booty. We may perceive in all these enterprises the expansive energies of the English at
work, we may perceive in them also the pressure
of accumulated capital, seeking lucrative investment. England was growing rich. But we must
recognize all these good things as the fruits of
peace. And it was Elizabeth who kept the peace, in
the face of all kinds of pressure from those immediately about her, at the expense often of the most
transparent breaches of faith, to the despair of her
counselors, her diplomats, her soldiers and her
sailors—nevertheless she kept the peace. More than
that, she managed to establish sympathetic contacts
with the rank and file of her subjects and to cre-
ate the tradition that she was the unique source of
all their blessings. Like her father before her, she
had a flair for popularity and she cultivated it care-
fully. It was her great achievement and perhaps
the chief source of her strength.

But during the years between 1572 and 1584
it had not been easy going. Not all Englishmen

were as secularly minded as their mistress was, not all of them prepared to accept peace and prosperity in satisfaction of all terrestrial and celestial requirements. There were the faithful Catholics who still demanded the consolations of their religion. Without the stimulus of a more active persecution than Elizabeth would countenance, their zeal in the late 60's was plainly flagging. The papal bull of excommunication did something, although not a great deal, to revive it. More potent was the influence of those English Catholic seminaries established on the continent for the education of English Catholic youths whose religion debarred them from the English universities. They began to pour a thin stream of missionaries into England in the mid 70's, and the stream thickened perceptibly when the Jesuits took a hand in the work in 1579. We get, in consequence, a definite reawakening of the Roman Catholic fighting spirit in England, which by the end of 1581 had assumed rather alarming proportions.

The issue was made all the sharper by the fact that while the Roman Catholics were attacking the Anglican establishment from one direction, a vigorous party among the Protestants was attacking it from the opposite one. These were the Puritans. They objected to the Anglican church on the

ground that it still contained too much that was
Roman in its composition. They disliked much of
the ritual, the church ornaments, the ecclesiastical
vestments and the whole episcopalian government. They complained about the indifference of
the clergy to their spiritual duties, called them
dumb dogs and idle bellies and demanded a
vigorous preaching ministry. They wanted to do
away with altars and images and painted windows.
They would have preferred a church government
after the Presbyterian model. But the great majority of them hoped and expected to secure all these
things by reform from within the church. There
were out-and-out Presbyterians and out-and-out
Separatists in the Puritan ranks who set up their
own churches "without tarrying for any," but they
were a small and relatively impotent minority.
The strength of Puritanism lay in those who accepted the Anglican establishment, believing that
they could amend it without destroying it. They
were sure that the truth as they saw it had only
to be stated in order to be embraced. We should
probably trace the direct origins of this movement
to those English Protestant refugees who had
established themselves in Switzerland and the
upper Rhine Valley during Mary's reign, and
who came home again after Elizabeth's accession

thoroughly saturated with the religious ideas of Calvin and the Swiss reformers. The Puritans were strong in the eastern and southeastern counties, very strong in London. They were strong also in the house of commons and they had good friends in the queen's council, notably the earl of Leicester, the royal favorite, and Sir Francis Walsingham, royal secretary. They were intelligent, competent, aggressive, and passionately loyal. That explains why their political influence was great in proportion to their numbers. To Elizabeth they were the one element among her subjects which she could count on to the death. But she did not like them and she did not like their notions. Particularly she disliked their insistence upon the powers and privileges of parliament and their leanings towards a more democratic form of church government. It was all of a piece and all fundamentally at variance with her own conceptions of the proper relations between crown and subject, church and state. She foresaw what her successor was to express that Presbyterianism and monarchy agreed as well as God and the devil. But she plainly could not afford to antagonize the Puritans when she needed every friend she could muster to face the menace from the Roman Catholics.

Elizabeth declined to believe that the papal bull of excommunication had turned all her Roman Catholic subjects to traitors and she was no doubt right, but the Jesuit ministers with one or two conspicuous exceptions were working hard to make them so. So was the captive Mary Stuart, so was the pope and the king of Spain and the Guisan party in France. And the consequence was that much against her will Elizabeth was impelled to adopt a very much more severe policy towards them. In 1581 she increased the fine for non-attendance at the established church from one shilling a Sunday to £20 a month, and she declared all Roman Catholic proselytizers to be traitors. Had these laws been rigorously applied, they would have spelled financial ruin for every Catholic layman and death for every Catholic priest. But they were mitigated to a considerable extent in execution. Actually, Roman Catholic laymen who kept clear of politics, and priests who adhered strictly to their religious ministrations generally escaped the full rigors of the law. Elizabeth was never concerned with what her subjects believed, but with how they behaved. She was not interested in saving souls from hell fire, but she was very much interested in the security of her realm. She persecuted the Roman Catholics because of their politics, not because of their religion. But it was not easy to differentiate in practice and it was not at all easy to convince the religious zealots of the sixteenth century that persecution of the faithful was not persecution for their faith. Elizabeth's Roman Catholic victims went to the gallows with the same sublime confidence that they were dying for God's truth, as had sustained the Marian Protestant martyrs through the fires of Smithfield. Whether Elizabeth liked it or not, the issue, as men saw it, was a religious issue and her severity towards the English Catholics simply served to stimulate their zeal and to arouse the crusading spirit among her Roman Catholic neighbors. There was active plotting against Elizabeth among the English Catholics, aided and abetted by the pope, the Guises, and the king of Spain, in 1582 and again in 1583. When the facts were discovered the Spanish ambassador at London was found to be deeply implicated. In January, 1584, he was invited to leave the country and diplomatic relations between England and Spain were once again severed.

Such was the state of affairs when the news of the assassination of William of Orange reached Elizabeth in the midsummer of 1584. It was plain enough that there was a dangerous amount of disaffection among the English Catholics and abundantly plain that Philip of Spain was definitely hostile. For ten years at least Elizabeth's Puritan counselors had been insisting that her one hope for safety lay in casting in her lot resolutely with the Protestant cause. There seemed to be no longer any reasonable doubt about it. Even Burghley, her most trusted adviser, and the leader of the peace party in her council began to waver. But it was a long and tedious business to bring Elizabeth to any warlike resolution. And the Dutch themselves were in two minds about seeking her help. They would plainly have preferred a French alliance and they did not formally approach her until after the French king had definitely refused their offer of sovereignty. Even then they were disposed to stand on terms. But the emergency was such as to admit of no delay and Philip of Spain did something to quicken her resolution by seizing all the English ships in Spanish harbors in the spring of 1585. Finally, in August of that year, she came to terms with the Dutch, agreed to take them under her protection and to send 5,000 foot and 1,000 horse to their assistance. They in turn contracted to repay all her expenses and to hand over three of their important port towns to her for security. Her military expedition under the command of

the earl of Leicester put forth for the Low Countries in December. Meanwhile the issue with
Spain had already been joined on the high seas.
In September, 1585, Sir Francis Drake with a fleet
of over twenty men-of-war had sailed with a royal
commission to attack the Spanish position in
America. But there was no formal declaration of
war and it was characteristic of Elizabeth that she
was seeking ways of coming to terms with Spain
underhand even before Leicester left England.

Leicester's expedition was not a success. He
lacked the qualities for a task which had tried all
the wisdom of William of Orange. He quarreled
with his subordinates, he quarreled with the
Dutch, and did what he could to sow dissension
among them. At the very outset he called down
upon his head the wrath of the queen by accepting
the post of governor-general without her consent.
He provoked the opposition of Burghley by careless and improvident financial management. He
even managed to antagonize Sir Francis Walsingham, the leader of the war party and his strongest
supporter in the English privy council. What he
and his generals accomplished against Parma on
the field of battle was negligible. Among other
disasters two English captains treacherously surrendered the towns in their charge to the enemy.

Individually the English gentlemen in Leicester's train displayed conspicuous gallantry and the most gallant gentleman of them all, Sir Philip Sidney, died as he had lived, magnificently. But it was not effective warfare. Indeed, Parma's military position was probably stronger when Leicester left the Low Countries in August, 1587, than when he first arrived there.

In any case, it was war. Whether Elizabeth admitted it or not, England knew and felt the necessity of setting things to rights within the gates. There were the Jesuit missionaries to be dealt with. They were given forty days to leave the kingdom or suffer as traitors. There was also Mary Stuart. In April, 1585, she had been transferred to the charge of Sir Amias Paulet, a stern and incorruptible Puritan, had been cut off from communication with her friends and had been placed under close surveillance. But loyal Englishmen were not satisfied. They realized that as long as she lived she would furnish a constant incentive to Roman Catholic uprisings in her favor. It was not a question of her guilt or innocence. Loyal Englishmen had tried and condemned her after the Ridolfi plot many years before and all that had happened since had simply served to emphasize her guilt. The problem was to bring Elizabeth to their way of thinking. It was with that end in view that Sir Francis Walsingham gave Mary a chance to communicate with her friends, secretly as she thought, but in such wise as to enable him to read every letter that came to her or went from her. He hoped in this way to get damaging evidence against her and he was not disappointed. A few months after the trap was set it caught evidence that a group of hare-brained English Catholics, led by Antony Babington, were plotting to murder Elizabeth, and were seeking Mary's blessing on their enterprise. Walsingham gave Mary time enough to endorse the plot and communicate the substance of it to her friends overseas; then he closed the doors, seized all of her papers, laid the evidence before his mistress and demanded that Mary be brought to trial. Elizabeth rather reluctantly consented. As for the trial it was little more than a formality. Everyone knew what the outcome would be. If the evidence against Mary had been far less convincing than it was, the result would have been the same. Mary was condemned not so much because of her complicity in the Babington plot as for her complicity in virtually every plot against Elizabeth during the eighteen years of her imprisonment, and chiefly because loyal Englishmen were agreed that she was a dangerous menace to the safety of their sovereign and their country, and that she ought to be got rid of. But that is not to say, as many of her friends have said, that the evidence against her was fabricated. There is no sound proof that it was, and every reason to believe that it was not. All that we otherwise know of Mary reveals the fact that she was quite ready to use any instrument which came to her hands to secure her release and destroy her rival. No one can blame her. Elizabeth had treated her abominably and Elizabeth was the enemy of everything she held dear. Walsingham might have fabricated the evidence, but he did not have to. All that Mary needed in order to plot against her rival was the opportunity. All that Walsingham had to supply was the opportunity.

Elizabeth hesitated some months after Mary was condemned to death before consenting to the execution. We may ascribe this to her fear of its effects on Scotland and on France. She was, at the moment, at war with Spain and it was no time to incur new enmities. It is to be noted that she seriously contemplated doing away with Mary by assassination, and, what is still more interesting, that there were many who believed that a private murder would have been less scandalous than a public execution. But she yielded at last to the pressure of her subjects and signed the death warrant early in February, 1587.

The closing scene of Mary's life was touching in the extreme. She walked to the block like a queen and like a queen she died. Nothing perhaps in her life became her more than the leaving of it. Certainly nothing in her life has so completely commended her to the admiration and sympathy of after generations. Yet, in pausing beside the grave of a very charming and a very unfortunate woman, one ought not to forget that she was in herself as great a menace as ever threatened the safety and welfare of England under Elizabeth. Loyal Englishmen breathed more freely after she had gone, and they turned with added confidence to face the overt enemy at their gates.

After Mary's death, Elizabeth, fearful of its effects, did her best to shift the responsibility of it on other shoulders. But she need not have troubled. Mary's passing scarcely created a ripple on the surface of European politics. France was not sufficiently interested to do anything about it, and James of Scotland did no more than enough to satisfy his subjects that he was not altogether indifferent to his mother's fate. As for the English Catholics, with the loss of Mary they lost their best hope, indeed their only hope of a Catholic succession. For James of Scotland inherited his mother's English claims and as between the heretic Elizabeth and the heretic James there was little to choose. What choice there was favored Elizabeth. So Mary's execution pretty well put an end to domestic conspiracies; at the same time it removed one great incentive for foreign invasion. In short, it strengthened Elizabeth's position very definitely.

She needed all the strength she could muster for she had news from Spain that Philip II was getting ready a great armada to attack her by sea. There had, in fact, been rumors of such an enterprise for more than a year and as early as January, 1586, Elizabeth had begun to make plans for the mobilization of her naval forces. But nothing came of it that year. Late in the fall Sir Francis Drake suggested an attack upon the Spanish coast, a private affair, privately financed, which would cost the queen nothing and commit her to nothing, but which might seriously derange the mobilization of the Spanish navy. Elizabeth liked the idea and Drake got away the following April with a fleet of twenty-two vessels, six of the queen's own ships among them. He managed to destroy virtually all the Spanish shipping in Cadiz harbor, and picked up a Portuguese carrack on the way home which sold for enough to pay all his expenses and allow a handsome profit to all his supporters. The whole exploit was magnificently audacious, magnificently successful. It was one more feather in Drake's cap, one more demonstration to him and to his seafaring fellows that they were easily the masters of Spain at sea. It dealt a shattering blow to Spanish morale and forced Philip to postpone the sailing of the armada for yet another year.

Elizabeth would have liked to believe that the postponement was to be until the Greek kalends. She had never been convinced that war was necessary, and she still declined to accept it as a fact. The enterprise in the Low Countries was producing nothing more than a constant drain upon her resources and when she came to consider it she asked herself why, after all, she was spending her money like water and wasting the lives of her best fighting men for the ungrateful Dutch. Her councilors insisted that it was a defensive measure and that unless she stopped Philip in the Low Countries she would presently have to face him on her own shores. But she was not at all sure that the reverse was not the case, and that Spanish hostility was not the result of her provocation. And as for religion, which seemed to be the chief bone of contention between the Dutch and their governors, what was their religion to her? After all, she claimed the right to establish her own church and it was hardly less than fair that Philip should be allowed an equal right to establish his. In short, Elizabeth was in a mood to consider terms of peace. Indeed, she had already begun to consider them. For something over a year different members of her council had been attempting to establish informal contacts with the prince of Parma through the medium of Italian and Dutch merchants. At one time there were no less than five such plans afoot at the same moment. They made relatively little progress, but they made enough to lead Elizabeth to believe that she might have peace on reasonable terms and they very perceptibly cooled her ardor for warlike courses. But she could not bring her Dutch allies to her way of thinking. They declined to participate in any formal negotiations with Parma. No doubt they realized that Elizabeth's conception of what constituted reasonable terms of peace was quite different from their own. She finally decided to proceed without them, and taking advantage of the friendly offices of the king of Denmark, she sent commissioners to Ostend in February, 1588, to negotiate with commissioners appointed by the prince of Parma.

Fortunately she did not altogether abandon her

warlike preparations. Peace she would have preferred and was prepared to promote but war she
seemed likely to get. Every dispatch from Spain
indicated that Philip's naval preparations were
proceeding steadily. Even Burghley insisted that
active measures should be taken for defense.
During the autumn and winter of 1587-8, English
shipyards were noisy with hammers and English
village greens were given over to the training of
armed men. Walsingham boasted in December,
1587, that through his labor and Burghley's,
26,000 footmen had been trained for the defense
of the coasts and 24,000 for a guard to the queen's
person, "a thing never put in execution in any of
her Majesty's predecessors' times." It was thanks
mainly to Sir John Hawkins, now treasurer of the
navy, that the queen's fighting ships were put in
first rate fighting trim.

In December, Elizabeth ordered her fleet to
take the seas under the command of her admiral,
Lord Howard of Effingham. Her plan at this time
was for Howard with the main fleet to guard the
Channel, while Drake with thirty ships proceeded
to the coast of Spain and did what damage he
might to the Spanish forces. But unfortunately
Drake could not get away promptly and while he
tarried, Elizabeth reached the conclusion that the

prospects for peace were fair and countermanded her orders. She reduced her crews to one-half their fighting strength and decided to abandon aggressive tactics, hold her forces in the Channel, and wait for Philip to take the initiative. It was bad strategy, but she could hardly do otherwise with her peace commissioners on the way to Flanders. The next month, however, brought more menacing news from Spain and the resumption of a bolder policy. And so the spring passed with Elizabeth constantly wavering between alternate courses, her councilors quite distracted, and her seamen tearing their hair. By some perversity of fate, the winds always seemed to blow fair for Spain when she blew foul, and set in hard from the south southwest when she blew fair. Those were the days when ships had to attend upon the weather as well as upon the royal whim.

Meanwhile her main fleet in good fighting trim held the seas off Plymouth, with a small squadron off Dover to prevent any sudden incursion from the Low Countries. And England was made ready for what almost everyone in England except the queen regarded as the inevitable struggle. It was rather a stupendous task to muster, drill, and equip an army of some 50,000 men in a country long unused to war, and with all its seasoned soldiers in the Low Countries and in Ireland; and to provide powder, shot, and supplies for a fighting fleet, the numbers of which were being augmented daily by converted merchantmen from the port towns. And besides that, money had to be found to meet the heavy drain upon the treasury, and France had to be watched on one flank and Scotland on the other, and the Roman Catholics had to be disarmed and their leaders placed under surveillance. The detailed work fell upon Burghley and Walsingham and, all things considered, they did wonderfully well. When the blow fell, England had a fleet of nearly 200 fighting ships and an army of sorts, though one wonders how these raw levies, the target of the London wits, would have stood up against Parma's Spanish veterans if they had ever got across the Channel.

The Spanish Armada was sighted off the Lizard, July 19, coming up the Channel with a favoring wind. It numbered about 130 ships as against about 200 in the whole English fleet, although in total tonnage there was not much to choose between them. But the English ships were more seaworthy and much quicker to the helm and able to sail much closer to the wind. They also carried heavier metal, arranged for broadside fire. Both in seamanship and in gunnery, the English had a decided advantage. The Spanish conception of naval warfare was born of smooth Mediterranean waters. Their objective was to grapple with the enemy and decide the issue by hand to hand fighting. On that account they carried more soldiers than sailors. The English, schooled on the rough Atlantic, had quite a different conception. With them it was long range gunnery and seamanship, ship against ship, not regiment against regiment. In the nine-day running fight up the Channel which followed, the English, having got the weather gauge at the start, were able to impose their own tactics, to avoid close quarters and to pound the unwieldy Spanish galleons at long range. There was never really any serious doubt about the issue, not in the minds of Drake or Hawkins at any rate. Had they coördinated their efforts more effectively and had they not run short of ammunition when they finally got the Spanish in a position for a mortal blow, they might have wiped the Armada off the seas.

The Spaniards seem to have had two objectives in mind; one, to establish a military base on the Isle of Wight, the other, to effect a junction with Parma in the Low Countries and hold the narrow seas long enough for him to convey an invading army to England. They failed in the first and anchored in Calais Roads hopeful of accomplishing the second. Thence they were driven away in panic by English fire ships and the next day had to accept battle on very unfavorable terms off Gravelines. After eight hours of fighting, in which the English sunk four ships and captured a number of others, the Spaniards turned tail. They narrowly escaped disaster on the Zeeland sand banks and fled away northward with the English at their heels. But Howard and his captains had exhausted their ammunition and supplies and could not support another engagement. So the Spaniards got clear away, north of Scotland and west of Ireland and so back to Spain again. Some forty of them were wrecked upon the Scottish and Irish coasts and scarcely half of them ever reached home.

The medal struck to commemorate the victory bore the legend, "God blew with his winds and they were scattered," but the winds did no more than complete the work which Howard and his captains had begun. It was English gunnery and English seamanship, applying to the purpose a more efficient type of ship, that really did the trick.

From the point of view of sea power, the defeat of the Armada marks the passing of the scepter from Spain to England. It marks also the definite reëstablishment of England as a first class power, a position which she had won for herself under Henry VIII and had lost again under Edward and Mary. But its most important effect was upon the temper of the English people. It established their faith in themselves and their pride in their country. For thirty-odd years they had been living in fear—fear of the pope, fear of Spain, fear of Mary Stuart, fear of conquest by the whole combination of forces which goes by the name of the Counter-Reformation. And now that fear was banished, and with it the tension which had held the national mind and national energies in check for a whole generation. And Englishmen became once more sure of themselves, sure of the superiority of their breed, boisterously sure of the power and greatness of their devoted land. We get the full flavor of it in Shakespeare's jubilant patriotism; particularly in those historical plays which he wrote in the decade following the Armada; best of all perhaps in Henry V's speech before Harfleur:

> On, on, you noble English!
> Whose blood is fet from father of war-proof;
> Fathers that, like so many Alexanders,
> Have in these parts from morn to even fought,
> And sheath'd their swords for lack of argument.
> Dishonor not your mothers; now attest

That those whom you call'd fathers did beget you.
Be copy now to men of grosser blood,
And teach them how to war. And you, good yeo-
    men,
Whose limbs were made in England, show us here
The mettle of your pasture; let us swear
That you are worth your breeding.

It is a new and forward-looking England, eager
for new conquests, new discoveries, great enterprises. In the fifteen years following the Armada
we feel ourselves for the first time in the Elizabethan age proper.

The defeat of the Armada seems for the
moment at least to have delivered even Elizabeth
herself from her cautious defensive attitude and
to have attuned her mind to vigorous, aggressive
warfare. The broken Spanish fleet had hardly got
back home before plans were afoot in England for
a descent upon the Spanish coast. They were
fathered by Sir John Norris, perhaps the most distinguished English soldier of the time, and by Sir
Francis Drake. The immediate aim was destruction and plunder but the plan early identified
itself with the efforts of Don Antonio, the Portuguese pretender, to establish himself on the Portuguese throne. In this latter regard there are faint
foreshadowings of the strategy which England was

[213]

to develop later with conspicuous success in the Peninsular campaign. The project took the form, not of a national, but of a private enterprise, largely financed by private adventurers with the queen as a contributor. It was adopted. The preparations for its realization proceeded through the winter and early spring of 1588-9. When the expedition finally set forth in March, 1589, it had assumed magnificent proportions—150 ships and nearly 20,000 men. It struck first at Corunna and did a good deal of damage to the shipping there, but failed to capture the town. Thence it proceeded south to Lisbon, its principal objective. It was now in Don Antonio's country and its leaders were hopeful that Portugal would rise against the Spanish government in his favor. That hope proved illusory; the racial and religious differences which supplied the foundations for the Dutch revolt were both lacking in Portugal and there was no restless bourgeoisie to build on. Lisbon was not taken and it was apparent that without heavier artillery, could not be taken. Meanwhile the crowded ships in the hot climate were collecting a heavy toll of disease and death. There was nothing to be gained by protracting the campaign. Drake thought of running down to the Azores on the chance of catching the Spanish plate fleet from the Indies, but the weather was too bad. The expedition which had set forth so gloriously in April limped back home late in June a mere wreck of an armed force. Some estimates placed its losses in human lives as high as 11,000 men. It brought no plunder to speak of. It had revealed the defenseless character of the Spanish and Portuguese coasts and had dealt a shrewd blow at Spanish prestige; but considering the leaders, the efforts put forth and the lack of any serious opposition, the positive results were meager in the extreme. If the Spanish Armada of 1588 had demonstrated that Spain could not conquer England by sea, the English Armada of 1589 had pretty well demonstrated that in the face of virtually no resistance the English could hardly make a dent upon Spain by sea. The results of this first venture in aggressive warfare were certainly not of a character to tempt Elizabeth to persist.

For the next five years her sea fighting was confined to the business of destroying Spanish shipping and interrupting Spanish commerce. A great number of expeditions put forth from England with these limited objectives in view. Most of them were private ventures, operating under some sort of a royal commission. Some of them are hardly to be distinguished from pure piracy. In some of them the queen herself participated. They picked up an enormous number of Spanish prizes, but the largest prize of all, the Spanish plate fleet from the West Indies, carrying the annual output of the Mexican and Peruvian mines, escaped them. It is curious that the Elizabethans never, in spite of all their efforts, captured a single one of these treasure ships. They had rather better luck with the great Portuguese carracks, loaded with spices and other precious merchandise from the East Indies. In 1592 a single one of these yielded over £100,000. How much in the way of income Elizabeth secured from enterprises of this sort is past finding out, probably more than enough to finance her part in them, but certainly not enough materially to increase her revenues.

The individual engagements almost without exception vindicated the superiority of the English gunners and the English seamen. There is record of only one of the queen's ships being captured by the Spaniards and the story of that capture is one of the great glories of English naval history. Sir Walter Raleigh has told it in immortal prose and Lord Tennyson in immortal verse. It was the story of the last fight of the *Revenge* in which Sir Richard Grenville for fifteen hours, until the last grain of powder was spent, stood off a Spanish fleet of 53 men-of-war and would have sunk his ship e'er he surrendered if his crew had not over-ridden him. It was magnificent, even if it was not war, and the tale of it stirred Elizabethan sea-farers like a trumpet. Such a defeat against such odds was worth a thousand victories. The Spaniards had no such tales to tell, and they lost in morale as heavily as the English gained. They lost also in the interruption of their commerce, even in neutral vessels, for the English claimed and exercised the right to seize all contraband of war bound for Spain, and they defined contraband of war in such broad terms as to include not only munitions, but also foodstuffs and ship supplies. This policy got England into a lot of trouble with her neutral neighbors, but she maintained her position nevertheless, and although she did not even attempt to establish a systematic blockade of Spanish ports, her men-of-war and her privateers intercepted a good deal of Spanish-borne com-merce which embarrassed Spain not a little. In 1591 the fear of capture by the English forced Philip to the desperate expedient of suspending the annual shipment of treasure from the West Indies, which came near to disrupting the whole Spanish financial system.

In 1595 Elizabeth was tempted to support an

expedition of more ambitious dimensions to the West Indies, chiefly with the idea of seizing the treasure fleet nearer its American base. Drake and Hawkins were in joint command. They quarreled, delayed, gave the Spaniards too much time to prepare for them, and in the end accomplished nothing of moment. Both of them died in West Indian waters and were buried at sea, a sadly impotent conclusion to the two most brilliant careers in Elizabethan naval history. Somehow Elizabeth never learned that unity of command was essential for success in any enterprise. The game she loved to play at her council table of pitting faction against faction could not be made to work on the quarter-deck or the battle field. But she repeated her mistake again and again. It may have been deliberately intended to prevent competition for the unique place she held in the affections of her people. Popularity was the one quality which she could not tolerate in her servants, least of all popularity based on such essentially masculine attainments as military success.

The West Indian expedition of 1595 was followed the next year by another expedition to the Spanish coast. It was prompted, apparently, by rumors of another armada preparing in Spain against England, and by an insignificant Spanish raid on the coast of Cornwall the previous summer. Its most active promoter was Robert Devereux, the young earl of Essex, who had succeeded his step-father, the earl of Leicester, as royal favorite. Essex, indeed, was the leader of the war party in the queen's council at this time. He represented the new, confident, adventurous spirit of the second generation of Elizabethans and although he found it hard to transmit his warlike ardor to his aging mistress, this time he succeeded, notwithstanding old Burghley, now in his seventy-third year, and Burghley's clever little hunch-backed son, Robert Cecil, who had become principal secretary.

The objective of this so-called Cadiz expedition was on paper at least, almost identical with that of the expedition of 1589, to wit, to destroy ships and stores in Spanish harbors, to capture and lay waste coast towns and to pick up all the plunder that could be picked up whether on land or sea. Essex and Lord Admiral Howard were in joint command. Essex himself cherished a secret purpose to seize and fortify a Spanish town and use it as a base for further operations against the Spaniards, but this was no part of the official plan. Expenses were underwritten in part by Essex and Howard as private adventurers, in part by the queen. When the expedition finally got away early in June, it numbered nearly 150 ships all told and carried over 10,000 fighting men. It included a squadron of 18 Dutch men-of-war supplied by the government of the Low Countries, a fact of significance as indicating that the Dutch rebels were now strong enough to carry their war against Philip II to his very doorstep. The expedition sailed straight for Cadiz, captured the city after two days' fighting, and spent the next two weeks in a systematic sacking of it. Of the ships in the harbor two great galleons were captured, the rest escaped or were destroyed to avoid capture. The Spanish losses in ships' cargoes alone are said to have exceeded ten million ducats. It was enough, in any case, to force Philip II into bankruptcy for the third time. How much the English secured in the way of booty cannot be precisely known. One estimate placed it at £170,000 but most of this went into the pockets of the soldiers and sailors. The queen and the adventurers hardly got enough of it to meet expenses.

The Cadiz expedition aroused Philip of Spain to action. For some years he had been contemplating another attack upon England. In the autumn of 1596 with what for him was amazing celerity, he organized, equipped, and dispatched a second armada. His plan this time was to establish himself in Ireland, but it was never realized. Once more "God blew with his winds and they were scattered," this time before they even got clear of the Bay of Biscay. Out of a fleet of 90 vessels more than 30 were lost. The rest put back into Spanish ports badly battered, and it was evident that nothing more could be done that season. But the expectation was that Philip would try again the following spring. Elizabeth was naturally alarmed and even old Burghley advocated a counterattack. The outcome was the so-called Islands voyage. It set out from England under Essex's command in June of 1597. It was about the same size as the Cadiz expedition the previous year, but different in this important respect, that it was a governmental enterprise, financed out of public funds; different also in that Essex was in sole command. Like the Cadiz expedition, it included a Dutch contingent. Its objective was very much the same,—primarily, of course to destroy the Spanish fleet, but after that plunder, notably East Indian carracks and West Indian plate ships. There was some notion also of establishing an English base in the Azores. In the end it accomplished none of these things, although it came nearer to capturing the West Indian fleet with ten million pesos on board than England was ever to come again. The whole affair was a dismal failure and it damaged the prestige of Essex not a little, although bad weather was more to blame than bad leadership. It was Elizabeth's last great naval effort. Philip II died the next year, and on sea, at any rate, barring always the incessant privateering, the war between England and Spain was virtually abandoned, although formal peace was not made until after Elizabeth's death. The fact was that the game proved to be hardly worth the candle. The damage done to Spain by the three expeditions sent to the Spanish coast was insignificant, the plunder secured not sufficient to meet the expense involved, the fame achieved doubtful at best. To the young gallants about the queen, the pomp and glory of war was its own justification, but Elizabeth looked for a more concrete return on her investment. Towards the end of her reign, what with wars in Ireland, wars in the Low Countries, and wars in France, the problem of ways and means became an increasingly serious one for her. Naval enterprises always offered a reasonable chance of profit and could generally be financed in part, at least, by private adventurers. For that reason, probably they appealed to Elizabeth. But as one after the other of them showed a loss, she became more and more reluctant to participate in them. She needed her money for other more pressing demands. It is probable also that the diversion of Essex's energies to Ireland had something to do with the matter. He, more than anyone close to Elizabeth, had promoted these expeditions. With the withdrawal of his interest, natural enough after the dismal failure of the Islands voyage, there was no one at court sufficiently influential to overcome the reluctance of Elizabeth to any new war-like enterprise.

Meanwhile, on land, Elizabeth had been engaged for some years on three fronts, in the Low Countries, in France, and in Ireland. In the Low Countries she was bound by treaty to maintain a force of 5,000 foot and 1,000 horse, and to supply adequate garrisons as well for the two "cautionary" towns of Flushing and Brill. A small English army was thus established in the Low Countries which was to remain there until 1616 and to serve as a training school for a whole generation of English soldiers. After Leicester had withdrawn in the spring of 1587, Lord Willoughby took command and after him, in turn, Sir Francis Vere and his brother, Horace. Sir John Norris and his two brothers saw long service there, and Sir Philip Sidney and his brother, Robert, and Essex, and Pelham, and North, and Conway, and that fiery little Welshman, Roger Williams, the original, very

likely, of Shakespeare's Fluellen, and many other
fine soldiers like them. They fought well and they
worked hard and they studied warfare in a truly
professional spirit. The story of their military
operations belongs rather to the history of the Low
Countries than to England. They coöperated on
the whole very well with the Dutch and made a
definite, although not a brilliant, contribution to
the Dutch fighting strength. It is probable that the
Dutch really needed them much less in the 90's
than they had in the 80's. In point of fact, Hol-
land and Zeeland were making a good profit out
of the Spanish war, chiefly because their command
of the sea enabled them to divert to Amsterdam
and Middleburg much of the commerce which
had previously gone to Antwerp and other parts
of the Netherlands which remained loyal to Spain.
But the Dutch were nothing if not thrifty and they
naturally welcomed English assistance on terms
which immediately, at any rate, cost them nothing.
They were, to be sure, under contract to repay
Elizabeth's expenses when the wars were over, but
that obligation rested lightly on their shoulders.
As for Elizabeth, she held the "cautionary" towns
in pawn, which also cost her money, but which she
dared not relinquish. She was conscious that there
was small profit in these Low Country enterprises,

for her or for England, and that the Dutch were exploiting her rather mercilessly. She was in that position which contemporaries liked to describe as having the wolf by the ears. But at least her Low Country contingents supplied her with a small nucleus of trained English officers and soldiers which she did not hesitate to draw upon when she had need of them elsewhere.

Elizabeth might have borne the burden of the Dutch wars with more equanimity if she had not found herself more and more deeply engaged in the civil wars in France. The last of the Valois kings of France was murdered in 1589 and the throne passed by right to the heretic head of the House of Bourbon, Henry of Navarre. Catholic France, led by the House of Guise and assisted by an alliance with Philip of Spain, was prepared to dispute that title. And so France, like the Low Countries, became a battleground of the contending creeds, with Spain once more the champion of the Counter-Reformation. It was plain enough to Elizabeth that Henry of Navarre could not be allowed to fail. The interests of England were just as much at stake in the battles against Spanish domination in France as they were in the Dutch wars or in the sea fighting. So it was that she was induced in 1589 to lend both men and money

to the French king. Between 1589 and 1595 she
sent no less than five expeditions to northern
France—perhaps as many as 20,000 men all told,
at an expense of at least £300,000. She has been
criticized for not doing more, but when it is recalled that she was maintaining a land war against
Spain on three fronts and financing unprofitable
maritime enterprises against the Spanish empire
at the same time, that her total annual revenues
probably did not exceed £300,000, and that she
had to dispose of a considerable proportion of her
capital assets to make both ends meet, the wonder
is that she was able to do so much. There is more
justice in the charge that what money she did
spend was spent unwisely and improvidently, but
it is easy to be wise after the event. The war demands could not possibly be foreseen or budgeted
for. It was clear enough that much more money
was needed than England could possibly supply.
Borrowing, except on a modest scale, was out of
the question. The European money markets were
badly demoralized and most of them in the control of her enemies. Her subjects regarded government loans with suspicion, and although her
credit with them was a good deal better than it
had been under her predecessors, most of what
they were willing to lend had to be drawn from

them by some more or less thinly disguised form of compulsion. The only alternative was additional taxes and Elizabeth, supersensitive always to public opinion, had plenty of reasons to believe that any heavy addition to the burden of taxes would be the surest way to alienate the affections of her subjects.

In France, as in the Low Countries, the results of her military intervention were meager, to say the least. Her forces in Brittany probably did something to prevent the Spaniards from establishing a strong base there although they did launch one raiding expedition against the English coast from Breton ports. Her forces in Normandy were of some assistance to Navarre in his Norman campaigns although not enough to prevent Parma from raising the siege of Rouen or the Spaniards from capturing Calais. Perhaps the great value of English troops in France as in the Low Countries was in giving concrete expression to "the common cause" as it was called at the time, and of creating a certain *ésprit de corps* among the three Protestant protagonists. This proved to be strong enough to prevent Henry of Navarre from abandoning the English and the Dutch when he decided in 1593 to abandon the Protestant faith and led to the conclusion by treaty of a definite triple alli-

ance in 1596. Henry, to be sure, negotiated a separate treaty with Spain two years later, but by that
time Philip II had shot his bolt in France and his
great general, Alexander of Parma, was dead in
the Netherlands and the Spanish colossus had
pretty well revealed itself to be but a colossus of
clouts, after all.

During the critical ten years following the defeat of the Armada, the important thing was to
keep the allies fighting, and fighting together, and
Elizabeth played her part, rather reluctantly and
on the whole rather ingloriously, but still effec
tively in bringing that to pass.

Henry IV's peace with Spain at least relieved
Elizabeth of any further expense in the French
campaign. That relief came betimes, for she had
presently to throw all the money and all the troops
she could spare into the business of coping with
rebellion in Ireland.

Space does not serve for more than the most
cursory survey of the perennial Irish problem as it
revealed itself under Elizabeth. The situation
there, roughly, was that of a district comprising
most of Leinster and known as the Pale, which was
governed by English officials, with a parliament
after the English model and with English law;
and outside of that the rest of Ireland, still in a

barbarous or semi-barbarous state, under clan chieftains and the Irish law. Henry VIII had made some effort to unite these two hostile groups by drawing the Irish chieftains into a feudal relationship under English law. He had also set up his new church there, had dissolved the monastic establishments as he had done in England, and had distributed their lands to the Irish chiefs. For the time, Ireland accepted his arrangements, but they had no roots.

The real trouble was that the English government set out to govern Ireland by English methods, in the English interest, and for English profit. No recognition was given the fact that Ireland had its own law, its own language, its own institutions, different to be sure from the English, but fitted to the temper of the people and adaptable perhaps to the uses of an orderly state. Quite the contrary! The Irish pretty frankly had the choice of abandoning their Irishry or of being treated as mere cumberers of the ground. As time went on, the policy of exterminating the native and handing his land over to English immigrants, steadily gained in favor. It would have simplified Elizabeth's problem considerably if she could have abandoned Ireland to its own devices. That she could not do, for the simple reason that Ireland lay too close to her doorstep and offered too convenient a base of operations for her enemies. The Irish chieftains, with any sort of foreign support, were always ready to strike at the English government. Elizabeth had to deal with them, she had to try to control them if only in self-defense. On that account, her government, not being strong enough to impose an English system of law and justice upon the wild Irish without distinction, was forced to the expedient of mixing in Irish inter-tribal and intra-tribal quarrels, of supporting faction against faction and of finding itself in the end without friends beyond the shadow of the Pale. The alternative, extermination, more or less in the manner applied later in America to the native Indians on the frontier, began under Mary in the so-called plantations of Leith and Offaly and was later extended to large parts of Munster. In this wise many gallant English gentlemen, notably Devonshire men like Raleigh and Carew and Grenville and Gilbert, got a stake in the country and a financial incentive to assist in the business of "civilizing" it.

Had Ireland been in any real sense a nation, it might have put up a stern fight, but it lacked any unifying principle, except perhaps a common hatred of the English and even that was not strong enough to prevent the Irish chieftains from seeking English assistance in their quarrels with one another. Religion offered another common bond. The Irish, so far as they were anything Christian, were Roman Catholic almost to a man, but they were no zealots. The absence of any disposition on the part of the government towards religious persecution gave them almost no opportunity to be martyrs. Yet, in the long run, it was religion more than any other force which was instrumental in arousing something like a united fighting spirit against the Elizabethan rule. And this was due to the missionary enterprise of the Jesuit priests, to men like David Wolfe and Nicholas Sander. Space does not serve to describe their devoted labors. In an amazingly short time and despite almost insuperable obstacles they accomplished really remarkable results.

It would be a gross exaggeration to say that a united Ireland, informed by genuine religious fervor, resulted from the work of the Jesuits, but they did kindle a spirit and a purpose in the Irish which almost for the first time in Irish history raised them above the level of mere clan interest. It was at the prompting of the Jesuits that James Fitzmaurice Fitzgerald in 1569 appealed to the pope to take Ireland under his protection and offered the sovereignty of their afflicted land to any Catholic prince whom Philip of Spain might appoint. And Fitzgerald tried to organize a national uprising on a Roman Catholic, anti-English basis. He failed in his immediate purpose and was ultimately forced to flee to the Continent. But he did succeed in inducing Pope Gregory XIII to dispatch two separate military expeditions to Ireland, in 1578 and in 1579. The first of these never got beyond the Strait of Gibraltar; the second, unofficially assisted by Philip of Spain, established an Irish base on the coast of Kerry and had the effect of stirring up a considerable amount of rebellion in Munster and Leinster. It came in the end to nothing, but it revealed the danger and invited a repetition. Thereafter Ireland occupied a very important part in virtually all of Philip II's hostile plans against England. It was very definitely the objective of his ill-fated armada of 1596 and was invaded in force by the Spaniards in 1602.

It was not until the last decade of Elizabeth's reign that she was faced with anything like a really dangerous Irish uprising, though she had to deal throughout her reign with sporadic rebellion in every province. On the whole she gained ground, enlarged the borders of the Pale, established Eng-

lish rule pretty securely in a large part of Munster, and set up some kind of government even
in Connaught. The one region in which she had
made least headway was in the north, in Ulster,
the land of the O'Neills and the O'Donnells. For
over thirty years her deputies had managed to
neutralize danger from that quarter by playing
one clan against the other and by encouraging dis-
sensions within the clans themselves. But in 1593
Hugh O'Neill had established his supremacy over
the O'Neills and Hugh Roe O'Donnell over the
O'Donnells and they had settled their differences
by a marriage alliance. The two men were quite
different in type, but they were both competent
leaders and both ambitious to extend their power
to the utmost. Neither of them dreamed of a
united Ireland but both were opposed to English
rule and both were easily accessible to Jesuit and
Spanish intrigue. The consequence was that rebellion broke out in Ulster in 1595 and spread
rapidly into Connaught. Three years of warfare
followed, marked by indecisive engagements and
interrupted from time to time by hollow truces.
The Irish on the whole had the better of the fighting and in the midsummer of 1598 O'Neill won a
decisive victory over an English army, marching
to relieve a fort on the Blackwater. The effect of

the victory was tremendous, and had O'Neill acted promptly he could have marched unopposed on Dublin. He contented himself instead with sending a small force into Munster. Within a fortnight that whole province was in rebellion. By the end of the year 1598 English government in Ireland was virtually nonexistent outside the limits of the Pale. To make matters worse, Elizabeth knew well enough that the Ulster rebels were drawing support from both Rome and Spain. It was in the same year, 1598, that Philip II came to terms with Henry of Navarre and was given a relatively free hand to deal with England.

Such was the state of affairs in Ireland when the young earl of Essex landed there in the spring of 1599, with an army of something like twelve thousand foot and one thousand horse, the largest military force sent to Ireland in Elizabeth's reign. It was expected that Essex would proceed against O'Neill—or the earl of Tyrone, as we had better call him—at once. But the season was not suitable for campaigning in Ulster. So Essex turned instead to strengthen the English position in Leinster, Munster, and Connaught. He established strong garrison positions in these regions, stationed about ten thousand of his troops there and with the remainder advanced against Tyrone toward the end

of August. Tyrone evaded an engagement and
offered instead to parley. Essex, after some hesitation, agreed and the two leaders met in private
conference at the ford of Ballaclinch. What
passed between them is unknown, but Essex decided that Tyrone might be won without further
fighting to the queen's obedience, and proceeded
to arrange a truce. In view of the fact that
Tyrone's forces outnumbered his two to one, he
probably had no sound alternative. But Elizabeth
made it abundantly clear that she was dissatisfied
with his whole course of action and Essex decided
to run back to court and win her over to his views
by a direct personal appeal. He ignored the fact
that she had expressly instructed him not to leave
his command without her consent. What happened
when he reached England will be dealt with presently in another connection. He never came back
to Ireland and early in the next year Elizabeth
appointed Charles Blount, Lord Mountjoy, in his
place, with orders to resume hostile operations
against Tyrone. Mountjoy followed in general
much the same policy as Essex, but more deliberately and with more skill. After a year's campaigning he had reëstablished English supremacy in
the south and center of Ireland and had ringed
Ulster round with a line of fortified stations,

which pretty effectually curbed Tyrone's power for harm. It was at this juncture that substantial aid for the rebels arrived from Spain. Philip had promised it before. It was indeed the expectation of Spanish aid that had prompted O'Neill and O'Donnell to rebel in the first place. It came at last early in September, 1601, a fleet of thirty-three vessels with some forty-five hundred Spanish troops aboard. They landed at Kinsale, just west of Cork harbor, proceeded to fortify their position, and called to Tyrone and O'Donnell to support them. Mountjoy got there first and laid siege, to be besieged in turn by a larger force which arrived a little later under the Irish chieftains. Tyrone had the advantage of position, and had he been patient might have starved the English into surrender. He decided to attack instead and was decisively defeated. He withdrew to Ulster and the Spaniards in Kinsale were obliged to yield. Thereafter the war went steadily in favor of the English. Once again Mountjoy suppressed the rebellion in Munster and Leinster and once again carried the fighting into Ulster. Tyrone offered to submit on terms. During the summer of 1602 he sent to Mountjoy successive offers of submission. Finally at the end of the year he threw himself without reservation upon the queen's mercy. Elizabeth, much against her will, agreed to pardon him, and in April, 1603, he submitted. He was on his way to beg pardon from her in person when she died.

And so was accomplished the first real conquest of Ireland. It had been a terribly expensive business, both in money and in human lives. The Irish for the time being at least were beaten and starved into submission. They yielded to English rule because they were not strong enough to resist it, but they never acquiesced in it. The Elizabethan policy in Ireland was to make a desert and call it peace. It served the immediate purpose which was self-defense, but it came nowhere near solving the Irish problem. Rather it created the Irish problem. It furnished the pattern for English policy in Ireland for at least two centuries to come. To the short-sightedness of Elizabethan statesmanship as much as to any other single cause we may ascribe the fact that Ireland remains a thorn in the side of Great Britain to this day.

Meantime, while English sailors were sweeping the seas and English soldiers were fighting the queen's enemies in the Low Countries, in France and in Ireland, England herself, secure behind her sea walls, was developing swiftly in all the arts of peace. Not all the domestic problems which had troubled Elizabeth in the first thirty years of her reign had been solved, but they seemed at least on the way to solution. The specter of a Roman Catholic reaction had been laid by the defeat of the Armada. The Puritan movement, aggressive as it was, was kept within bounds by loyalty to the queen and devotion to the common cause. There were a few radicals among the Puritans who insisted upon an immediate reformation, and who organized themselves into Presbyterian classes and Separatist congregations. They laid the foundation for the English dissenting faiths, and one small group of them laid the foundation of a new England beyond the seas. But they probably represented a very small minority. Englishmen by and large accepted the Anglican church as a satisfactory solution to the religious problem, went to the established Church on Sundays and bent their abundant energies to secular pursuits.

England was still, like all the rest of the western world, an agricultural country, but faster than all the rest of the world it was becoming commercialized and industrialized. The last twenty years of the reign mark the real advance to her maritime supremacy, not only in sea fighting but also in sea trading. English ships, financed by English companies, plowed in increasing numbers the waters of every European sea, from Archangel in the far north to the Guinea Coast of Africa in the far south, and English trading enterprises had reached as far eastward as the Caspian Sea and as far westward as the coasts of Virginia and New-foundland. At the very end of the century the queen granted a charter to a company to trade with the Far East, none other than the great East India Company.

In the older regions of trade, much of what the English gained they gained at the expense of their old competitors, the Italians and the Germans. At the end of the reign of Henry VIII a large part of the English export trade was foreign borne. At the end of Elizabeth's reign, almost all of it was in English ships. It is to be noted that the Dutch carrying trade was developing about as rapidly as the English, but acute commercial rivalry between the two allies was deferred until the next century.

The bulk of the English export trade was still, as it long had been, in English cloth, and most of it still flowed through the old channels of the Merchant Adventurers. The Merchant Adventurers were indeed the most important commercial organization in England at this time and occupied a position in the Elizabethan world of business and finance analagous to that which the East India Company was to occupy two centuries later.

The interest in the cloth trade extended far below that of the trading class. It reached, in fact, into the country cottages, for cloth making had in large measure escaped old gild restrictions and had spread all over the countryside. Weaving and spinning both had become customary avocations for a large number of Englishmen whose main business was agriculture, and furnished an important part of their scanty incomes. On that account the continuing prosperity of the cloth trade was a matter of wide national concern. The disposition then as now was to blame bad business on wealthy malefactors and in periods of depression the trading companies had to face a good deal of popular criticism. The attack upon monopolies in Elizabeth's last parliament is to be attributed in part to this cause. But they rode out the storm and, except with France, overseas trade was officially at any rate confined to monopolistic companies for a good half century to come.

Not only were the old industries rapidly expanding but new industries were rapidly developing. Space does not serve even to enumerate them. Many of them, like the alum and salt industries, owed their rather phenomenal growth to the amazing development of coal as a commercial fuel. Coal mining in the last quarter of the sixteenth century plays a part in English commercial and industrial development comparable to railroad building in the fourth and fifth decades of the nineteenth century. It came betimes, for England had almost exhausted her supply of wood fuel.

In agriculture the enclosure movement, which has been dealt with earlier, went on apace, despite the efforts of the government to put a stop to it. In the main it was still for sheep grazing, though the rapid development of the towns created an increasing demand for foodstuffs which the older agrarian economy was hardly adequate to supply. It was easy to justify on economic grounds, and one Thomas Tusser even went so far as to sing its praises in bad verse. But it bore hard upon the agricultural worker and is to be directly charged with his progressive degradation which has been one of the major calamities in the development of modern England.

There is indeed a seamy as well as a fine side to those spacious later days of Queen Elizabeth. If the rich were growing richer the poor were pretty obviously growing poorer. The towns were pestered with beggars, the country roads full of roving bands of unemployed, rogues and vagabonds, who begged where they could, stole where they might, and were ready to feed any kind of disorder afoot. One of the most serious problems which England had to face throughout Elizabeth's reign was this problem of poverty and it got worse instead of better as time went on. The old ways of dealing with it, by private charity, by the church, and by the towns individually, proved to be hopelessly inadequate. Finally Elizabeth undertook to define and impose a program of poor relief for England as a whole. We need not stop to consider its provisions. They did not accomplish what they set out to accomplish. The poor are still with us and like to be. The significant fact is that the Elizabethan poor law of 1597 definitely recognized poverty as a national problem and for the first time definitely attempted to deal with it comprehensively on a national basis. The national responsibility was then positively assumed and has never since been denied. Thereafter it was a matter of ways and means, of national policy, not of national obligation.

But the dominant note in the last decade of Elizabeth's reign was not poverty but prosperity. England was then, if ever, forward-looking, confident, sure of itself and sure of its great destiny. This was notably true of middle-class England

and it was middle-class England that really mattered. The great figures were all middle-class, the soldiers and the sailors, the merchants and the men of affairs, the statesmen, the artists and the men of letters, all middle-class. And fortunately they had a middle-class queen. Had it not been so there would have been trouble and to spare in the closing years of her great reign. For this new England was not to be driven, not even to be led except by a leader thoroughly in sympathy with its plans and purposes. And this new England did not hesitate to speak its mind. It had its legitimate channel of expression in the house of commons and more and more as the reign progressed the commoners came to regard themselves as the mouthpiece of the nation on questions of public policy. They had not hesitated to speak out frankly early in the reign on the question of the queen's marriage. They did not hesitate, notwithstanding royal commands to the contrary, to insist upon the importance of settling the difficult question of the succession. They criticized freely Elizabeth's ecclesiastical arrangements and her fiscal arrangements and in the very last parliament of her reign they denounced in unmeasured terms her wholesale creation of monopolies. She scolded them, threatened them, disciplined them, but she never broke with them, and whether she resisted their pressure or whether she yielded to it the final word was always one of affectionate coöperation. Englishmen might cherish many grievances against her government but they never cherished for long any grievance against herself. One gets the impression always that behind all the incidental bickerings there was deep and abiding confidence, love and loyalty to the queen on the part of her subjects and to her subjects on the part of the queen. She gave voice to this in almost her last public utterance. "Though God," she said, "has raised me high, yet this I account the glory of my crown, that I have ruled with your loves."

But Elizabeth's love was a jealous love and the one thing she could not tolerate in any of her servants was popularity. It was Essex's strong bid for popularity which more than anything else was the cause of his undoing.

It will be remembered that he came back from Ireland in the autumn of 1599 to justify his course of action there to the queen and to win her support. After their first interview, which was inconclusive, Elizabeth declined to see him again. Indeed after that interview she never did see him again, alive or dead. For eight months she kept him banished from court and virtually in confinement and then brought him to trial. The charges against him had to do with his conduct in Ireland and with his disobedience in leaving his command without royal consent. He was found guilty, suspended from his public offices, and ordered to remain prisoner in his own house at the queen's pleasure. Later he was deprived of some lucrative monopolies. But the heaviest of all his punishments was banishment from the royal presence. For Essex owed all that he had to Elizabeth's personal affection for him and he realized clearly enough that all he could ever hope for depended upon the recovery of that affection. He did what he could by correspondence, but got nowhere. His one chance lay in a direct appeal and that Elizabeth steadily denied him. It is hard to explain her attitude except on the grounds that she feared that her emotional interest in him would lead her to betray the public interest. Essex was insolent and disobedient, hard to control; he was also the most popular man in England. He had taken advantage of every military enterprise in which he was engaged to strengthen his popularity among the gentry by wholesale conferring of knighthoods. He had too many friends and adherents in the house of commons, he had too large a following among the Puritans. It was rumored that he was in correspondence with James

of Scotland, the heir presumptive. It was rumored
also that the army in Ireland was at his command.
In short, he was potentially at any rate too strong,
too independently strong. Elizabeth, like all the
Tudors, wanted her servants to be completely dependent upon her favor. Essex's insolent behavior
often conveyed the impression of indifference to
her favor. He was heard to say that her character
was as crooked as her carcass. Elizabeth herself
declared that her purpose in exiling him was to
break his proud spirit, and that explanation seems
to fit better with the known facts than any other.
In any case it failed, for Essex after a year and a
half of submissive banishment from court began
to contemplate a bolder policy. His plans, so far as
he had any, were to remove those whom he conceived to be his enemies, notably Robert Cecil and
Walter Raleigh, from about the queen and to
reëstablish himself in her favor. His friends began
to gather at Essex House in such numbers that it
presently became apparent that something un-
toward was afoot. The privy council, in February,
1601, ordered him to appear before it and explain.
He pleaded sickness, refused to go, and proceeded
to gather his supporters together for some positive
action. Once again the privy council intervened
and sent the lord keeper, the lord chief justice

and two others to inquire what he was about. He locked them up in his study and set forth with about two hundred of his friends and followers to arouse the city of London. He banked heavily upon his popularity and hoped and believed that the populace would flock to arms in his support. But they did no more than cheer, and the city officials made haste to oppose him. In the end, after some quite futile street fighting, he slipped down to the river and got back by boat to his house again. There he was presently besieged by the queen's troops in force and obliged to surrender at discretion.

His trial and execution followed. It may be admitted that he had cherished no treasonable purpose against the queen or the state, but the case against him was quite strong enough to justify the sentence. We need not ascribe it to an old woman's wounded vanity or suppose that his fate might have been different if a ring of magical potency which he is supposed to have sent Elizabeth had ever reached her. No doubt her vanity was wounded, but no doubt also Essex had revealed himself on many counts to be a dangerous enemy to her government as she conceived it and would have it. Reduced to its lowest terms, his immediate intention was to force her to discharge his enemies from her council and to be governed by his friends. In many respects his effort resembled that of the duke of Norfolk some thirty years before, except that it was based rather upon the Puritan left than the Catholic right and directed against Cecil *fils* instead of Cecil *père*.

How far beyond that he would have gone had he been successful in his first step there is no way of knowing. But it was known that he contemplated using the Irish army and perhaps securing further aid from Scotland. We should perhaps in judging him distinguish between what he actually did and what he dreamed of doing. But taking them both together they constituted a pretty damnable indictment. He was a gallant gentleman but a very ungovernable one and by the standards of his time he deserved to die as he did.

His death saddened the aging queen and it saddened her people, who, rightly or wrongly, had come to regard Essex as the national hero. But they did nothing about it except to damn Cecil and Raleigh in song and story. Politically it cleared the air and reëstablished the integrity of the privy council which for ten years had been split in twain by the rivalry of Essex and Cecil. Thereafter Robert Cecil, the clever little hunchback, ruled without dispute. Elizabeth herself was nearly seventy,—still vigorous, still ready to display her dancing to foreign ambassadors, but by all human calculations not far from the end. Those around her began to think about her successor, began to look away from the sun setting to the sun rising. Some talked of Lord Beauchamp, the representative of the Suffolk line, some of Arabella Stuart, the daughter of Darnley's brother, some of the earl of Huntington. The Roman Catholics put forward a rather fantastic claim for the Spanish infanta, Isabella. But most men agreed that James of Scotland was the only possible successor, and Robert Cecil the next year began secretly to establish his connections in that quarter. Elizabeth herself remained noncommittal and her councilors did not dare to broach the subject to her until she was in the article of death. At the very end, she is said to have named James to succeed her.

Elizabeth died on the 23d of March, 1603, and courtiers raced each other to the Scottish border to carry the news to James. Her passing marked not only the end of her reign, it marked also the end of her dynasty. Indubitably she was a great queen, but her greatness was not of any conventional pattern. She was not a great leader of her people but she was a wise and careful guardian of them with a sure instinct for their real interests. Lytton Strachey has put the matter in a nut-shell: "The fierce old hen sat still, brooding over the English nation, whose pullulating energies were coming swiftly to ripeness and unity under her wings. She sat still; but every feather bristled; she was tremendously alive."

It would be hard to point to any evidence of constructive statesmanship in her whole performance. To keep the peace within and without her borders and to give Englishmen a free field in which to realize their own purposes, that was her great achievement. Very little originated with her and she changed very little. Her method of government was to utilize old Tudor machinery in theory, making such amendments in practice as the exigencies of the particular situation seemed to demand. It would be hard to say what her views were upon such fundamental questions as the allocation of the law-making power or the taxing power in the state. She was not given to political theorizing and she resolutely avoided general commitments. Hers was a rule of thumb method which depended entirely for its success upon her own personality. It was getting pretty evident towards the end that the new wine was too potent for the old bottles, but she did nothing more about it than to loosen the corks a little. The great achievements of her reign lie outside the court circle and must be looked for in the theater and in the marketplace. But she got the glory of it all, and not unfairly so, for if she did not in any sense initiate it she made it possible. She brought England through a very perilous passage into smooth waters. Unfortunately for her successors the chart by which she steered her erratic course was destroyed with her death.

FINIS

BIBLIOGRAPHY

THERE are two good biographies of Henry VII,
one by James Gairdner (London, 1889), the other
by Gladys Temperley (London, 1918). The best
life of Henry VIII is by A. F. Pollard (London,
1913). On Edward VI there is nothing better
than the introduction to his *Literary Remains*
(Roxburghe Club, 1857) by J. G. Nichols. The
most complete life of Mary is by J. M. Stone
(London, 1901). J. E. Neale's *Elizabeth* (London, 1934) has displaced all the earlier short lives
of her, though there are some brilliant glimpses
of her personality and her court in Lytton
Strachey's *Elizabeth and Essex* (London, 1928).

On the social life of England in the 16th
century, the best book is *Shakespeare's England*
(2 vols., Oxford, 1917). Trade and industry are
well treated in E. Lipson, *The Economic History
of England* (3 vols., London, 1915, 1931); the
agricultural problem, particularly in its social im-
plications, in R. H. Tawney, *The Agrarian Problem in the Sixteenth Century* (London, 1912).

The history of English literature in the 16th

[253]

century is best surveyed in vols. iii-vi of *The Cambridge History of English Literature* (14 vols., Cambridge, 1907-16). The chapters on England in J. W. Allen, *A History of Political Thought in the Sixteenth Century* (London, 1928), give easily the best presentation of that thorny subject. For political institutions reference may be made to A. F. Pollard, *The Evolution of Parliament* (London, 1926), Kenneth Pickthorn, *Early Tudor Government* (2 vols., Cambridge, 1934) and to the introductory notes in J. R. Tanner, *Tudor Constitutional Documents* (Cambridge, 1922). W. S. Holdsworth, *A History of English Law* (9 vols., London, 1922-6), is the only good book on the development of English law under the Tudors.

There is an enormous literature on the religious issues under the Tudors, most of it pretty heavy reading. For those who want the facts the volumes by James Gairdner and W. H. Frere in *A History of the English Church*, edited by Stephens and Hunt (London, 1902, 1904), are as serviceable as any.

In general the volumes by H. A. L. Fisher and A. F. Pollard in *A Political History of England* (London, 1906, 1913) provide the most scholarly presentation of Tudor politics. But no one should miss J. A. Froude's classical account of the period from 1529 to 1588 (12 vols., London, 1893).

There is a pretty complete survey of all the pertinent literature on Tudor England in Conyers Read, *Bibliography of British History—Tudor Period* (Oxford, 1933).

INDEX

THE NORTON LIBRARY HISTORY OF ENGLAND

General Editors

CHRISTOPHER BROOKE
Professor of History, Westfield College,
University of London

and

DENIS MACK SMITH
Fellow of All Souls College, Oxford

Already published:

ROMAN BRITAIN AND EARLY ENGLAND, 55 B.C.–A.D 871
Peter Hunter Blair

FROM ALFRED TO HENRY III, 871–1272
Christopher Brooke

THE LATER MIDDLE AGES, 1272–1485
George Holmes

THE CENTURY OF REVOLUTION, 1603–1714
Christopher Hill

FROM CASTLEREAGH TO GLADSTONE, 1815–1885
Derek Beales

MODERN BRITAIN, 1885–1955
Henry Pelling

Forthcoming titles:

THE TUDOR AGE, 1485–1603
Margaret Bowker

THE EIGHTEENTH CENTURY, 1714–1815
John B. Owen